THE LUCID EXPRESSION OF THOUGHT

A History of the Birmingham &
Edgbaston Debating Society
1846 – 2006

A man approaching 40 (!!!) should
read something educational. You
will enjoy this. You are
remarkably successful & we are
very proud of you. Keep your
feet on the ground & your eye on
the ball. That way you will
keep notching up the scores in the
game of life. Love you
always.

Dad.

x o x

THE LUCID EXPRESSION OF THOUGHT

A History of the Birmingham &
Edgbaston Debating Society
1846 – 2006

Charles Wade

First published by
History into Print, 56 Alcester Road,
Studley, Warwickshire B80 7LG in 2006
www.history-into-print.com

ISBN 1 85858 310 1

A cataloguing in Publication Record
for this title is available from the British Library.

Typeset in New Baskerville
Printed in Great Britain by
Cromwell Press Ltd.

CONTENTS

FOREWORD

The story of the Birmingham & Edgbaston Debating Society has been interwoven with that of the city of Birmingham itself for the last 160 years. As current president of the society, I am proud of the fact that we have sent 15 Members of Parliament to Westminster, five of them becoming Privy Councillors and one a Prime Minister. Many other members went on to be Mayors and Lord Mayors of Birmingham, and to play an important part in the commercial life of the city. Most of them joined the society as young men because they understood that the ability to express themselves clearly, and to think on their feet, is an essential capability in business, the professions and politics. If the society has given them that, it has performed a valuable service.

I am most grateful to Charles Wade for writing this history of the society, to Conrad Charles who has helped him with research into the society records, to Bill Caswell who took responsibility for raising the finance for the project, and to the many other members who have provided their recollections of the past and present.

When the society was formed in 1846, the days had not long passed when any form of debating club was regarded as dangerously seditious by the authorities! However, it has survived and prospered, and it remains in good health 160 years on. Long may it continue to attract people who are interested in 'the lucid expression of thought'.

Jim Fergus
President 2005-06

ACKNOWLEDGMENTS

The primary source of information for this narrative has been the minute books of the society and the other papers that have been deposited at the Birmingham Central Library. In the early days, the minutes were kept to the bare facts. More recently, debates have been reported almost verbatim. Whilst this might be seen as going to the other extreme, it would have been fascinating to have known exactly what a group of predominantly young and politically educated men thought about the Corn Laws, the Factory Acts and Chartism when these were the big issues of the times. The author has made his judgments based on the clues that are available.

Many members have assisted the author including the 'father of the house' Kenneth Wilkinson who joined the society in 1950. He was a fighter pilot in the Battle of Britain in 1940 and his memories stretch back almost ten years further back than anyone else's. Others such as Roger Stone and Tony Grazier went the extra mile to help fill in the gaps from 1960 onwards.

Amongst others who have helped are Mrs Mollie Martineau, Donald Wasdell, John Masterton, Jim Fergus, Stephen Gilmore, Reg Willsher, Tim Ryan, Geoffrey Oakley, Tony Ridgway, Raymond Burton, Geoffrey Burcher, Ian Marshall, Anthony Joseph and Andrew Peet. Thanks are also due to Alison Smith and David Bishop in the archives department of the Birmingham Central Library, and to Maggie Burns in the Local Studies and History Section.

Whilst the committee of the society has considered, on several occasions recently, ways of getting a book written and published, it was Bill Caswell who took the initiative and approached me. He pointed out the interesting coincidence that the Leamington Tennis Court Club, of which I had written a history, had also been formed in 1846. He also raised, from members and other sources, the necessary funds to publish the book.

However, one person without whose help it would not have been possible for me to write this book is Conrad Charles. He has acted as researcher and spent a lot of time at the Birmingham Central Library exploring diligently the society's records and other sources of information.

The society itself is particularly grateful to those who have financially supported the publishing of this book:

PROLOGUE

The story of the Birmingham & Edgbaston Debating Society is a *continuum* of the story of the Edgbaston Debating Society which was founded in 1846. Although the latter was to amalgamate with the Birmingham Debating Society in 1855, it was in reality a takeover by Edgbaston. The Birmingham society, which was the second to be formed, might otherwise not have survived. The first Birmingham Debating Society was, like Edgbaston's, founded in 1846, but it lasted no more than four years. Very few records exist of the first and second Birmingham societies and this makes it difficult to write about much of their activities in the pre-amalgamation years. The jubilees and centenaries celebrated by the society in subsequent years have all been taken from 1846 rather than from the date of amalgamation.

From the outset, a stated objective of the Edgbaston Debating Society was 'to train members in the art of clear thinking and the lucid expression of thought'. Debating societies have always provided an opportunity for their members to practise their speaking skills in front of a live audience. If anything, this is more important to many of the participants than the debate itself or the winning of it, particularly to the ambitious young bent on self-improvement. They soon learn that rhetoric is a skill that has to be learnt and practised. There may be a few naturals speakers and debaters around, but they are very much the exception. They too would not want to squander their gifts by lack of preparation and rehearsal. Whilst all this leads to a better level of performance, it does not always help the debate itself. Prepared speeches will be delivered as soon as their proponents catch the chairman's eye and they are unlikely to stray much from that which they intended to say, whatever the thread of the preceding argument.

The choice of motions is always important in a debating society and they have usually covered the burning political and social issues of the day. The author has reminded readers, in the course of this narrative, of what those issues were. However, some abstract motions began to be debated towards the end of the nineteenth century and increasingly from thereon. They have borne the brunt of a certain amount of criticism ever since as such motions lack focus, allowing speakers to interpret their meaning in any way they choose. If there is no agreement about the meaning of a motion, many of those participating in the debate do not know which side they are on and probably don't even care. As a result, the ambiguity itself becomes an issue and wit matters more than profundity. It could be suggested that abstract motions are more inclusive than political, philosophical or literary subjects that require knowledge of the subject, but cleverly contrived wording and punning in the framing of motions does not always disguise their vacuity. The present arrangement is that the debates secretary submits a list of motions to the society's committee for consideration. It is clear that, at the present time, some of its members prefer light and topical issues for debate and react with less enthusiasm to what they might describe as 'heavy' subjects. Perhaps a balanced diet is the best solution.

Nonetheless, a debate benefits from passion and that is more likely to be encountered when a political issue is discussed, rather than an abstract motion. The political loyalties of the society are more one-sided today and this makes it difficult to find issues that divide the house somewhere near the middle. This was less of a problem when the society was formed, even though it was dominated by Liberal sympathisers, many tinged with Radicalism, rather than by Tories. Then, anyone in the educated and enfranchised elite of the nation could be a Whig/Liberal or Tory/Conservative supporter without raising eyebrows. The governing elite was content that gentlemen faced gentlemen across the floor of the House of Commons. However, the society became increasingly Conservative as the nineteenth century progressed and, after the demise of the Liberal party in 1916, Labour supporters in the society's membership were few and far between.

The Oxford and Cambridge Unions provide teeth-cutting opportunities for undergraduates seeking careers in politics. They both pre-date the Birmingham & Edgbaston Debating Society and are closer to the parliamentary model. Amongst rebellious undergraduates a divided house is easier to achieve. There has been passion and uproar in many of their debates and none is better remembered than the Oxford Union's 'king and country' debate in 1933. The result became international news.

In the early days of the Edgbaston Debating Society, and then of the Birmingham & Edgbaston Debating Society, the proposer was allotted an hour for his opening speech and summing-up. The majority of his allotted time would be used for his opening speech. The opposer could speak for 45 minutes, but was not allowed to sum up. Contributions from the floor were allowed 15 minutes. As a result, there were few speakers in debates and those that did were well prepared. Impromptu contributions were a rarity. The style of speaking was different to that of today: wordy to the point of prolixity and with many literary allusions. But the long speeches in the early years of these societies only reflected the times and how it was done in the House of Commons. The sort of two-hour philippic that might have come from Palmerston or Gladstone is no longer fashionable and would today exhaust the patience of listeners adjusted to taking in their political messages in short digestible sound bites.

The proceedings in a council chamber or in the House of Commons provided the model for the society. Long speeches were expected and discussions in those days were on serious topics. Speakers in society debates had to know what they were talking about, whether it was Palmerston's foreign policy or the economic consequences of Corn Law repeal.

During the latter half of the nineteenth century particularly, a number of cities organised mock parliaments and these were a variation on the debating society theme. They have disappeared now, but at least one Prime Minister, the Glaswegian Andrew Bonar Law, used them to hone his debating skills. The Birmingham and Edgbaston society was used in a similar way by another future Prime Minister, Neville Chamberlain and, a generation earlier, by his father Joseph who, whilst not quite reaching the top of the 'slippery pole', was very close to it in spite of changing parties.

The university unions, school debates and mock parliaments follow the House of Commons format in that the opposing sides of the argument sit facing each other. Participants in a debate are then expected to sit on the benches of the side that they support. They are then given opportunities at intervals during the debate to cross the floor in the manner of the *pedarii* in the Roman senate. In this way the chairman is able to call speakers from each side alternately, and the ebb and flow of support can be seen. This adds an extra confrontational *frisson* to the proceedings. At present, the Birmingham & Edgbaston Debating Society begins its proceedings with a dinner and the members remain in their seats for the debate. The business of the evening is held back until the plates and cups are cleared away. The average age of those present today is far higher than it was in the mid-nineteenth century and the format of the evening probably suits the majority of members.

The two-valued orientation of debate does tend to polarise positions. One is asked to take sides on the presumption that there is only a choice between two sides: either for or against. Debate does not readily allow a multi-valued orientation on an issue and it is the latter that charts, in the political or business context, the course towards a compromise solution which works. But a debating society enjoys debate for its own sake and its decisions do not have to be implemented. The affirmative and negative proponents exaggerate their own claims and belittle the arguments of the opposition, and this does not allow that a matter of opinion is never one hundred percent true or one hundred percent false.

The American writer and physician, Oliver Wendell Holmes, in his *Autocrat of the Breakfast Table* published 150 years ago, used a simple hydrostatic fact to illustrate the weakness of the two-valued orientation in debate: 'If you have a bent tube, one arm of which was the size of a pipe-stem, and the other big enough to hold the ocean, water would stand at the same height in one as in the other. Controversy equalises fools and wise men in the same way - and the fools know it.'

Anyone involved in a heated discussion, when opinions diverge, will know exactly what Holmes meant. One can find oneself arguing against positions of faith, or opinions that are stated as facts. There comes a point when views expressed are so bigoted or prejudiced that all moderation is driven out and civilised people would rather change the subject than be drawn in any further. The discipline of debate, subject to formal codes of behaviour, is better for all concerned.

The society, of course, does not make political decisions and, in the final analysis, the results of its debates do not change the nation's course. But that particular truth has to be suspended, just as it is in all sporting contests, in order to bring the competitive instinct into play. Without it, games enjoyed by amateurs and debate with nothing financial or consequential at stake would become pointless. The framers of motions should seek controversial issues that raise the temperature. In the nineteenth century the motions for debate, whether religious, philosophical or political, were signposts to the issues of the day. It would be a pity if this were to change.

Another innovation that began in the late nineteenth century was the impromptu debate which requires that nobody is given advance notice of the motion. It still happens today once in every session (the debating 'season' from September to May), but the Victorian forebears organised it in a more stimulating way. Then, all the speakers from the floor were called by the president in a random order and were told whether they had to speak for or against the motion. There is no better training for anyone, particularly the prejudiced, than to be obliged to speak against his or her own convictions. And all those present had to concentrate on the ebb and flow of the argument in order to contribute meaningfully to it.

Since the Edgbaston and first Birmingham Debating Societies were formed separately in 1846, there have been momentous political events such as the repeal of the Corn Laws, the political duel between Gladstone and Disraeli, the debates on Home Rule and the Parliament Act, the 1914-18 war and the demise of the Liberal party, the financial crisis of 1931, the rise of Nazi Germany and another war, and then the post-war period which will probably seem relatively stable in retrospect to those who live 100 years hence. All this is reflected in the motions chosen for debate and helps us to chart the society's political loyalty moving from Liberal to Conservative, where it almost certainly still resides. Like many other bodies, the society has had its great days and not so great, but it has survived and should continue to do so for as long as the intellectual challenge of debate is enjoyed.

Many distinguished men have been members of the Birmingham & Edgbaston Debating Society including 15 Members of Parliament, one of them a Prime Minister, a number of mayors and lord mayors of the city, in the days when the mayor was the man in charge, several judges, councillors and chief magistrates. This is something of which the society can be proud.

CHAPTER 1

1846 was a critical year in the history of the nation. A second failure of the potato crop caused great distress in Ireland. The Repeal of the Corn Laws led to the fall of Sir Robert Peel's ministry. There was also distress in France owing to bad harvests, and Louis Napoleon escaped from Ham prison.

In order to understand why a group of young men living in Edgbaston, a small residential town on the outskirts of Birmingham, should have wanted to form a debating society in 1846, we need to recall something of their aspirations and what life was like for them at the time. They were mostly in their early twenties or even younger and could look forward confidently to careers in business or the professions. In many cases they would have been following in the footsteps of their worthy fathers who had already started companies or professional practices in Birmingham, a rapidly growing conurbation that would soon swallow Edgbaston and other nearby villages.

At almost the same time as the Edgbaston society was formed, another debating society was being planned in Birmingham itself and it is impossible to know whether this was a coincidence, or if the businessmen of Birmingham believed that they ought not to be upstaged by their smaller and socially superior neighbour. The records of the short-lived first (1846-50) and second (1850-55) Birmingham societies are scanty compared to Edgbaston's and the reader is asked to understand that this narrative follows the happenings of the Edgbaston society in its early days, until the eventual amalgamation, unless stated otherwise.

There was nothing unprecedented about forming debating societies in Birmingham. The first of them had been the Robin Hood Free Debating Society in 1774. It met at the Red Lion public house in the Bull Ring, the very heart of the town. This was soon followed by the Society for the Encouragement of Free and Candid Disputation. In 1789, the Society of Free Debate was formed and, in 1792, it chose to debate whether Brutus was justified in killing Caesar. With the republican ideals of the French Revolution attracting some support at that time, the debate generated much emotion and riotous behaviour, and the magistracy was called upon to intervene. The society's meetings were interdicted on the grounds that, in view of the riots, public discussion of dangerous subjects should be discouraged. In the last two decades of the eighteenth century the authorities were concerned about anything that they construed to be seditious. The battle for free speech had not yet been won.

Those who governed Britain were paranoid about the spread of French revolutionary ideas and it took a lengthy war and many years of peace afterwards before the deep suspicion of radicalism in any form subsided a little. But by 1846 political attitudes had changed and a few young men who lived in Birmingham and Edgbaston decided that the time was right to form new societies. They had been little more than children when Queen Victoria had come to the throne nine years earlier. In some cases their fathers, to whom they would have deferred, might have thought that there was nothing unreasonable about the 'Peterloo Massacre' or transporting the 'Tolpuddle Martyrs' in chains to Australia. The Tories, of course, felt more strongly about such things and they had dominated the government of the nation for several generations. However, the first members of both debating societies came from Liberal families, rather than Tory, and a few of them might have had radical tendencies which they would soon have shed. They had their own career ambitions and were not seeking to overturn the established order. They also had a sense of civic duty that, for the Edgbaston society members, would have been focused more on Birmingham, where they worked, rather than Edgbaston, where they lived. Those who wanted to commit themselves to public service, as well as to their careers in business or the professions, would have set their sights on municipal politics. They would almost certainly have regarded ambitions to sit on the benches of the House of Commons as being beyond their reach. The Reform Bill of 1832 had allotted Birmingham only two Members of Parliament: previously it had had none at all. However, within 30 years, a member of the debating society was able to make the transition from municipal to national politics and to achieve high office and fame. In the next 100 years, another 14 other members of the society were to follow him to House of Commons.

The 1832 Reform Bill would not have enfranchised the younger of the men who formed the debating society as they lived in their fathers' households and being a householder was an essential qualification for the franchise. Nonetheless, they took an interest in national politics and this becomes evident from the motions that were debated. Not to have a vote would have been frustrating for them, and whether Great Britain could claim to be a democracy, with only a small minority of the population enfranchised, was an arguable point. It is possible to conclude that the formation of a debating society was driven by a certain amount of political and social impatience with what had now become the early Victorian patriarchal society. In fact, debating societies were being formed everywhere in the country at this time.

In the nineteenth century Edgbaston was under control of the Gough-Calthorpe family which owned much of the land and refused to allow factories and warehouses to be built there. As a result, Edgbaston avoided the decline of other Birmingham suburbs from middle-class spaciousness and dignity to the noise and dirt of manufacture and the crowding of an industrial population. As a residential area, it was as desirable in the mid-nineteenth century as it is now. Edgbaston eventually became part of Birmingham, by which time there was no longer any farmland separating it from its dominant neighbour. The population of Edgbaston in 1846 was about 8,000 and this number would have included many who were in domestic service.

The household of a typical Birmingham business or professional man would have included a living-in manservant and maid, a cook and a groom. The groom might have worked on a part-time basis or have been shared with the neighbours. The best houses in Edgbaston today might have cost £300 to £500 in 1846. The men who lived in them would have managed comfortably on £300 per annum, but probably enjoyed a higher income than that. This applied more to the fathers of the young men who founded the debating society than to the young men themselves. They would have enjoyed the benefits, and perhaps the frustrations, of living in the family home until marriage at a relatively young age.

For those who lived in Edgbaston, but had business in Birmingham, the daily journey to their places of work would have involved a ride on horseback or in a horse-drawn carriage of some type. The roads between centres of population were macadamised by then and that would have included the road from Birmingham to Bristol which would have been used for part of the ride from Edgbaston to what today would be called the city centre, although Birmingham then was not a city in status. The other part of the route would have been through green fields or improving minor roads. The journey itself would not have taken long and, with no traffic problems then, it would have been accomplished in less time than it takes today in the rush hour. Bad weather, particularly in the winter months, would have detracted from the enjoyment of the open road in an unheated carriage, but men were made of sterner stuff then.

The first members of the Edgbaston Debating Society walked, rode on horseback, drove themselves in two-wheeled one-horse gigs or chaises or were driven more grandly by their coachmen or grooms in a barouche, landau or phaeton. Hotels, public houses and other places of assembly had facilities for looking after their guests' horses and carriages. Being able to afford some sort of personal transportation was a pre-requisite of living in a place like Edgbaston. Food, stable rent and other costs for one horse would have amounted to £35 per annum. Adding the cost of maintaining a gig in good repair would have taken the costs above £50 per annum. This represents a relatively high proportion of income, but not greatly different from that of car ownership today. Even with the invention and development of railways, horse-drawn transportation continued to grow throughout the century and more and more people became 'carriage folk'. It was ultimately to be the internal combustion engine, not the railway, which brought about the eventual disappearance of the privately owned horse-drawn carriage.

In the previous decade the better roads had led to well-organised public transportation by coach between most towns of any size. It would have been possible to journey from Warwick to Stratford upon Avon, for example, in less than an hour. The network was well organised and timetables were adhered to. This mode of transport could only be afforded by some of the population and it was the railways that brought relatively low-cost universal travel.

By 1846 the railway boom was in full swing. It now took less than five hours to cover the 97 miles to Liverpool and a little less for the 120-mile journey to London. This was much quicker than the 12-hour journey by stagecoach. New Street Station was commissioned at this time, but it was not the first terminus in the city. That was in Curzon Street. Others at Snow Hill and Moor Street soon followed.

As rail travel became much easier, people living in or around Birmingham could visit nearby towns such as Worcester, Bewdley or Tamworth. Until then most of the population never ventured anywhere away from where they were born and bred. The first rail excursion organised a decade earlier by the travel company, Thomas Cook was from Loughborough to Leicester, a journey of little more than ten miles. Yet it is said that nearly everyone who bought tickets had never been to Leicester in their lives! As well as the main lines connecting the big cities, local lines made it possible to live in Ladywood, Moseley, Harborne or Handsworth, and to work in the centre of Birmingham. A railway station was to open in Hagley Road, Edgbaston, in 1874 and another in Somerset Road in 1876.

Improvements in modes of travel did not impinge on the working classes at all. They were expected to work long hours in the factories - their political weakness and *laissez faire* economics left them little choice - and they lived near their places of work to which they walked. They might have left their rural homes in what was a time of agricultural depression to find work and higher wages in Birmingham, and a journey back to the places from whence they came to visit families and old friends would have been a rarity.

By any measure Birmingham was a major British city well before 1846 and the eventual granting of a Royal Charter fifty years later only served to confirm what was already an established fact. The emergent and increasingly wealthy middle-class which chose to live just outside the centre of Birmingham in Edgbaston was worthy and industrious, and worked long hours. But recognising the dangers of all work and no play, the younger men began to think of ways that would give them a reason to meet and socialise. Their thinking was influenced by the fact that a good education was considered to be one of the marks of a gentleman and, conscious perhaps of their relatively humble antecedents, they cared about self-improvement. Developing rhetorical and forensic skills, and being well informed, could only help that process.

There were no cinemas in 1846, no television broadcasting, no wine bars, no health clubs, no golf clubs, with two or three exceptions, and virtually no clubs of any type for sports or games. Excepting cricket and golf, most of the games that are enjoyed today hadn't been invented. All forms of football were in their crude infancy and the only racquet games played were Tennis (known since as Real Tennis when Lawn Tennis, which was not invented until 25 years later, became universally popular) and Rackets (which had developed during the mid-eighteenth century in the debtors' prisons). The landed gentry hunted, shot and fished, but the members of the debating society who lived in Edgbaston and worked in Birmingham were not landed gentry. The rural squires in the surrounding counties would certainly not have considered these worthy Birmingham citizens to be on the same social stratum as themselves. Being a gentleman had a different meaning then to what it did one hundred years later. It implied breeding and class, not a standard of behaviour. However well a man behaved did not make him a gentleman. However badly a gentleman behaved, he was still a gentleman. In today's classless society, the term has lost much of its meaning.

Some idea of class attitudes of the time can be learnt from a gentlemen's club, primarily for Tennis and Rackets, which opened only 25 miles away in Leamington Spa in the same year as the debating society was formed. The founding members of the Leamington club included a few noblemen and most of the others were country squires - all good men to hounds. They wanted something else to do and somewhere to congregate other than in their own homes. One of the nobleman at the club saw fit to blackball a doctor's application for membership on the grounds that he would not wish 'to meet someone socially who he might have to call in to visit him in the morning'. Nobody on the committee appeared to think that there was anything unreasonable about this and the doctor, a distinguished member of his profession by the standards of the time, remained blackballed. Seventy years were to pass before the Leamington club accepted a solicitor as a member.

The class divide between the Leamington club and the Edgbaston Debating Society had much to do with their respective locations: Birmingham and Leamington Spa were worlds apart. According to G.M. Trevelyan's *English Social History*, Victorian England at this time consisted of two strongly contrasted social systems, the aristocratic England of the rural districts and the democratic England of the great cities. The counties and market towns were still ruled and judged by country gentlemen to whom all classes bowed. But the cities were governed by a totally different type of person and in accordance with a very different set of social values.

Whilst medicine and the law were regarded as professions, they in themselves did not ensure respect. By today's standards, medicine was very basic in 1846 and solicitors were regarded with some suspicion, more Uriah Heep than David Copperfield. Many of Dickens's heroes were typical of the men who were members of the debating society, but not quite gentlemen. In one of his finest works, *Great Expectations*, we are asked to believe that Pip - lacking any breeding - could be accepted as a gentleman after a limited amount of instruction from Herbert Pocket. But Pip's benefactor, the convict Magwitch, could hardly have been expected to understand that. Pip, a blacksmith's apprentice, eventually might have passed at best for middle-class. At the end of the novel Pip took employment as a clerk. Being a clerk had more status then than it does now and he eventually became a partner in the business. But having to earn one's living at all was hardly the mark of a gentleman. The black and white 1940s film of *Great Expectations*, with the elegant John Mills cast as Pip, was a somewhat idealised interpretation.

The predominant choice of career of those who joined the debating society in its early days was the law. The fact that they were entering a profession rather than trade still did not open doors for them into the higher levels of society. Only the advocacy branch of the law, the church and service in the army were considered to be acceptable pursuits for a gentleman. But by 1846 the raffish Regency years had by now given way to outwardly more restrained behaviour, even if that involved a certain amount of humbug and hypocrisy. Birmingham's manufacturers were more concerned about making money than frittering it away like their supposed betters.

The terms *middle-class* or *working-class* were not used in the early and mid-nineteenth century, but the founders of the society knew exactly where they were in the social hierarchy. They were constrained from birth within a class structure in which the country gentry regarded anyone earning a living from trade as socially inferior. The founders of the debating society were Birmingham's finest, but they would never have been comfortable in the company of the landed gentry. In any case, they would have had little or no contact with the latter in 1846 and making money concerned them more. Birmingham had become known as a 'city of a thousand trades' or as a place where new settlers were attracted by the belief that one could 'get rich by nightfall'. The population was over 100,000 by 1831 and, by 1846, had passed 200,000. But it was gloomy, noisy and dirty, with slums that were a disgrace. Edgbaston somehow remained a residential enclave largely untouched by what was happening in the city. Even there, nonetheless, as A N Wilson reminds us in *The Victorians*, the time traveller from the twenty-first century would notice the sweaty smells of the servants who never bathed, the nights with no electricity, the gas flares against sooty skies, the excellence of the rail and postal services, the smells of horse dung and straw, the toothache, the halitosis, the terrifying inadequacy of dentistry and medicine, and the acceptance of infant mortality.

The first members of the debating society would probably have had their secondary education at an endowed grammar school or a private academy of some sort. The fashionable public schools, such as Eton, Harrow and Winchester, were still few in number, but their imitators were to multiply in the middle of the nineteenth century. These establishments were intended to educate an elite, armed with a thorough knowledge of the classics, which would run the nation and its empire. This was just too late for the founders of the debating society, but not for their sons. Nonetheless, the choice of motions in the early days of the society suggest that the founders were well educated with an interest in historical matters, the arts and the classics, so their education was far from lacking and, in many areas of scholarship, was better than that of their equivalents today.

CHAPTER 2

The Street Commissioners ran Birmingham until 1851 and one of their last great undertakings was a sewerage scheme. They also were concerned about checking the output of smoke, particularly as manufacturing developed throughout the 1840s. A special inspector was appointed in 1844 to deal with steam engines and smoke generally. Gentlemen at this time wore narrow-waisted frock coats, high shirt collars and cravats.

1846 was an important year in the political life of the nation and was dominated by the repeal of the Corn Laws. Whilst this was to be the start of 30 years of prosperity, it split the Tory party and finally ended the dominance of the *ancien régime*, a process that had begun with the Reform Bill of 1832. The Tories were the 'gentlemen of England' and their leader and Prime Minister, Sir Robert Peel, recognised that the Corn Laws - measures intended to protect agriculture - had to be repealed because of the hardship they were causing the industrial masses which, at times, could not afford bread. Repeal was passed because over 100 Tories who supported Peel voted for it. The Peel supporters, who included almost everyone of cabinet rank in the party, joined with the Whig/Liberal opposition. Amongst them was William Gladstone. The Tory squires left behind probably decided that Peel, with a fortune made by his father from trade rather than through owning land, was not a gentleman after all. Nonetheless, he was the greatest man of his time. Peel's apostasy could not be forgiven by what was left of the Tory party. It was virtually leaderless in the House of Commons and this provided Benjamin Disraeli with his opportunity. That the Tory gentlemen came to be led by this somewhat raffish figure of Jewish descent is one of the most fascinating studies in political history.

The Reform Bill of 1832 would have been remembered by the most of the members of the debating society as something important that happened in their childhood or youth. The bill might have averted a revolution and it established the principle that the constitution is based on popular representation. It seems incredible today that sensible men could have denied this principle and argued instead that the King should invite whatever interests he thinks fit to send persons to Parliament to take counsel with him on the affairs of the nation. The Whig aristocrats who passed the

Reform bill did not believe in democracy, but they were prepared to concede a share of power to men of property. Everyone else, including the working-class, was left out. One consequence of this exclusion was *The People's Charter*. The rise of Chartism was regarded by the powers that be as revolutionary and its suppression was popular, yet five of the six key points in the Charter are now part of our constitutional system.

With £10 householders enfranchised, the nationwide electorate increased from 300,000 to 800,000. Whilst the increase amounted to no more than what the Whig administration wanted for its own purposes, the enactment of the bill meant that some of the founders of the debating society 14 years later were enfranchised. The passage of the bill had not shaken the aristocracy's hold on political power, nor was it intended to do so. The Whigs thought they had done enough for the foreseeable future. They did not consider for a moment that they had taken a step on the way to a universal franchise and would have been horrified by that realisation. 35 years were to pass before another reform bill was passed.

Birmingham had become one of the great towns of England by 1846, in population second only to London, but it did not become a city until 1889. The industrial revolution had created it. It was the city of the great partnership of Matthew Boulton (1728-1809) and James Watt (1736-1819) and their steam engines. And of William Murdock (1754-1839) who pioneered gas lighting and steam-driven transport. For almost 100 years the Street Commissioners ran the town until a town council took over in 1851. The Street Commissioners had been empowered by a local Act of Parliament: it had been realised a century earlier that large and rapidly expanding towns could not be controlled by medieval corporations and manorial courts. One of the preoccupations of those who lived in these days was disease and public health. The police force was in its infancy and so was street lighting. It is difficult to understand today that many on the town council with a Liberal disposition believed in *laissez faire* principles to an extreme degree in some cases. The freedom of an Englishman's home was paramount even if his drains emptied into somebody else's yard. This stemmed from a dislike of centralised government and a belief in individualism: perhaps a sentiment could be carried too far.

Birmingham's leading citizen in the mid-Victorian era was John Bright (1811-1888). He was born in Lancashire and had a Quaker upbringing. In 1840 he and Richard Cobden launched a campaign for the repeal of the Corn Laws. He became a Manchester MP in 1843 and, after losing his seat in 1857 because of his pacifism, he was adopted by the Liberal party in

Birmingham. He was a great orator and served in Liberal cabinets. He resigned because of the Liberal imperialist policy on Egypt, but remained an MP for Birmingham until his death. By then he had been eclipsed by an even brighter star in Birmingham's firmament, a Londoner who became Birmingham's best-known citizen of the nineteenth century: Joseph Chamberlain (1836-1914).

The political sympathies of the founders of the society were predominantly with the Whig and Liberal party. But political parties in those days were loose groupings and were not disciplined by whips. The Whig and Liberal combination would certainly not have considered itself to be a party of the left. Present-day observers of the political scene are conditioned to see everything in terms of right against left, with closely-knit political parties. In the middle of the nineteenth century, parties were held together only by shared interests and objectives and would disband and re-form if those interests or objectives changed. The twentieth century disciplined party model was unthought-of in this earlier era. Both sides of the house considered that they were gentlemen opposed by gentlemen. The Whig aristocrats owned vast estates and were a powerful force. They were allied to the manufacturing classes, owners rather than workers of course, and were more cosmopolitan than the typical Tory squire. The more radical Liberals realised better than the latter that some concessions had to be made to the new forces arising in the body politic, but they would not have gone so far as to embrace the full Chartist manifesto.

It was the Whigs who had introduced the First Reform Bill and they and their Liberal allies also believed in *laissez faire* economic policies that suited the aristocratic business interest. The party itself was a coalition of Whigs, who hitherto represented the great landowners and the moneyed industrialists with little interest in reform, middle-of-the-road Liberals, and Radicals who had objectives and philosophies that even their colleagues might have regarded as extreme. The protectionist Tories, or the 'country party', began calling themselves Conservatives. After the defection of the Peelites in 1846 the remaining Tories were united but denied power, whereas the Whig and Liberal combination formed the predominant governing coalition.

The changes in the names of the two main parties that occurred gradually through the nineteenth century were more than merely cosmetic. *Whig* and *Tory* were pejorative rather than descriptive names. The Whigs effectively disappeared as a political grouping in the 1860s. The name *Tory* today has survived because news editors and headline writers prefer a short word to a long one. The Liberal party's *laissez faire* economic policies would be considered right wing today. It was the more paternalistic Tories, or at least some of them, who were concerned about the exploitation of women and children in factories and a Tory philanthropist, the seventh Earl of Shaftesbury, who introduced the Factory Acts to protect them. The Whigs regarded these measures as unwarranted interference in freedom of contract.

The terms *left* and *right* had no currency in the mid-Victorian era. Even if they had, it is doubtful whether Tories like Peel or Shaftesbury would have considered themselves to be further right than Whig grandees such as Viscount Palmerston or Earl Russell. There were still large landowners in the Tory ranks and country squires on the Whig benches, so things were not clear-cut and it would be an over-simplification to try and make them so. Things became a little clearer as the century drew to its close. By then, William Gladstone's progression from Peelite Tory to Liberal statesman had changed the politics of the age. This culminated in the Liberal party being replaced by Labour in the twentieth century.

Birmingham's manufacturers would have regarded Shaftesbury's endeavours with a great deal of suspicion. They wanted to keep labour costs down and, whilst not quite evil in a 'Gradgrind' sort of way or as ruthless as the owners of coalmines, they resolutely pursued their own interests. The voters of the town gave their support almost exclusively to the Liberal candidates for parliament. It was to be some time before a Conservative represented a Birmingham constituency.

CHAPTER 3

After Peel's fall in 1846 Lord John Russell became prime minister. The distress in Ireland continued and relief measures were passed in the House of Commons. England and the USA settled the Oregon boundary question. There was tension between Great Britain and France over Spain.

The meeting that led to the formation of the Edgbaston Debating Society took place at the Birmingham and Edgbaston Proprietary School on 8th October 1846. The chairman for the evening was John Barlow and 22 in all were there. This we know from the minutes taken at the meeting, but we know little of the talking or correspondence that must have gone on before the meeting took place or why Barlow was in the chair. Numerous letters would have been written and carried by the highly efficient penny post, in some cases making five scheduled deliveries in a single day.

The names of those present were listed in the minute book in the order that they would chair debates, something that was settled by ballot at the meeting. As was the usual practice in the nineteenth century, the names in the list had only the title *Mr*, although initials were also used in a few cases. With everything recorded in long-hand, any abbreviation might have been welcomed by the minute taker but, more relevantly, the first names of those present might not have been known to the person taking minutes, nor to each other. A speaker at a meeting would have addressed a fellow member as 'mister'. To address another man by his first name in social intercourse would have indicated a close friendship or a familial relationship.

Further up the social scale, gentlemen addressed each other by surname only. The use of *Mr* in the minutes rather than the appendage *Esquire* provides an interesting clue to their place in the Victorian class system. Anyone who put *Esquire* after his name did so to indicate that he was a squire - the principal landowner in a rural community - or the younger son of a nobleman. *Esquire* conferred social distinction and using it without being deserving of it would have invited the ridicule of one's fellows. In the twentieth century *Esquire* became nothing more than an over-used *politesse* in correspondence and, consequently, has been rendered meaningless.

The 22 who attended the first meeting of the debating society were, in ballot order, Henry Martineau Greenhow, Herbert Wright, Edward Peyton,

Benjamin St John Matthews, Henry Elliott, William Thomas Greenhow, John Homer Chance, Thomas Martineau, John Chamberlain Barlow, William Elliott, Francis Owen Clark, William Ridout Wills, George Warden, Alfred Heyman Louis, Algernon Sydney Clark, Alfred Seddon Bolton, James Tertius Collins, Robert Francis Martineau, Francis Seddon Bolton, John Howard Clark, Edmund Kell Blyth and Edward Goddard.

The name Martineau appears in the list three times, twice as a surname and once as a second name because of a relationship by marriage. Henry Martineau Greenhow became an army surgeon and was to be present at the Siege of Lucknow during the Indian Mutiny. The brothers Thomas and Robert Francis Martineau were the sons of Robert Martineau, who was Mayor of Birmingham in 1846 and ran a brass foundry. Thomas Martineau (1828-1893) was 18 years old and Robert Francis Martineau (1831-1909) was a mere 15 years of age. They were both to make their marks in local government. Thomas Martineau became Mayor of Birmingham 40 years later (as were to be his son Ernest and grandson Wilfrid) and he was to be knighted. In 1852 Thomas Martineau was to enter into partnership with Arthur Ryland who had started a legal practice in 1828. The Martineau family were of Huguenot ancestry and became something of a Birmingham dynasty. They were Unitarians, a Nonconformist sect which was particularly active in Birmingham and provided some of the city's mayors and others prominent in local administration. Probably the best-known member of the family nationally was the journalist and short story writer Harriet Martineau (1802-1876). She was the aunt of Thomas and Robert Francis Martineau and lived in Norwich. Her writings expressed a complacent middle-class perspective on the times and that was exactly what her readers wanted, undisturbed by the appalling condition of the poor.

Herbert Wright became a Birmingham solicitor and William Greenhow a county court judge. John Barlow, the chairman of the first meeting, and William Wills became solicitors (Wills was later to be a judge), and Alfred Bolton was a Justice of the Peace. The new members included some manufacturers such as William Elliott whose company made fabric and linen buttons for garments. These replaced metal buttons and made Elliott wealthy.

Religious dissent and political radicalism became part of the Birmingham tradition and, as well as the Martineaus, the Kenricks, Nettlefolds and Chamberlains - all big names in the city's history in the years ahead - were also dedicated Unitarians. The Cadbury family were Quakers who, like the Unitarians, linked their religious beliefs to business and politics.

Only a few weeks after the Edgbaston society was formed the Birmingham Debating Society was founded on 3rd December 1846. John Winfield was elected as its honorary secretary and treasurer, but the records prior to 1848 have been lost and it is impossible to know whether he held these offices from the outset. The task of presiding over debates was taken in turn by the members. There was a 'Committee of Questions' comprising the secretary and two others. What its remit was apart from choosing subjects for debate is not made clear in the scant records. Nonetheless, this committee chose weighty political matters for discussion.

The young men who formed both societies wanted to learn how to speak well and the debating society would develop this aspect of their education. But what was it all for? Apart from anything connected with business, the only route to fame and fulfilment that they could see ahead was to make a mark in local government. As already mentioned, the Martineau brothers in the Edgbaston Debating Society, for example, were the sons of a man who was the mayor of Birmingham. The mayor was the leading citizen, of course, but would young Thomas Martineau have chosen his course in life out of filial duty? And would he have foreseen that it would lead to fame, albeit only locally, and a knighthood?

Things, however, were to change in the last half of the nineteenth century. Upward social mobility, from being very unusual, became a real possibility. Another even greater man was to follow the course set by Thomas Martineau. The achievements of Joseph Chamberlain, who joined the Edgbaston society a few years later, and his two sons, Austen and Neville, belong to the history of the nation. When Joseph Chamberlain was first elected to Parliament, nobody made an issue about whether he was by then a gentleman, whatever his private thoughts on the matter. Birmingham has reason to be grateful to dynasties like the Chamberlains, the Martineaus, the Kenricks, the Nettlefolds, the Cadburys and others who worked hard to build its civic pride. There were plenty of others prepared to take the money and run.

At the first meeting of the Edgbaston society, the laws of the society were approved. They were very similar to those of the Birmingham Debating Society which had been formed a few weeks later. It seems likely that one set of laws had been based on those of the other and the Edgbaston society, the older of the two by seven weeks, can claim to be the originators. Over the next few months, the Edgbaston society's laws were to be amended to rectify minor 'teething troubles'. Thereafter the process of amendment over the years was, as one would expect, a continual one. The laws were numbered by Roman numerals but, in due course, Arabic numbering was used. It was only relatively recently that the laws became referred to as 'rules'.

Notable amongst the Edgbaston society's laws was the stipulation that matters of theological character would not be debated. For the transaction of constitutional and organisational business, a quarter of the entire membership had to be present. This had to be amended eventually. Also, interestingly, only the opener in the affirmative could speak twice in a debate. His two speeches together were not permitted to exceed an hour. Anyone else could speak for a half-hour. The laws were written into the minute book and were followed by a list of 26 members who would, in succession, propose a subject for discussion. The last man named was the most recently elected member, Thomas Salt from Erdington, and his turn would be 18 months away.

The time allowed for speeches was, by today's standards, inordinately long. But then speakers were expected to be well prepared and knowledgeable on their subject. Unsurprisingly, only a few people - perhaps six to eight - spoke in the debates but, even so, one must assume that they did not all use their time allocation. The proposer had an hour in total to cover both his opening speech and summing-up added together, whereas the opposer was not permitted to sum up. Speeches of this length or even longer were nothing unusual in the political life of the nation in the nineteenth century. Today, speeches of any sort are expected to be succinct and free of too many literary allusions. Listeners just don't have the time or patience for anything else. In January 1849 there was a rule change to permit members to speak twice in a debate provided that the chairman allowed it. The law was amended with the words 'until every member desirous of speaking has done so'. This still did not mean that the leader in the negative was allowed to sum up, even if he could speak twice under the terms of this rule.

The day and timing of meetings were subject to frequent amendment in the following years. The first of these was to move meetings to every second Thursday. Times were moved forward to 'half past seven o'clock', and 'the debate shall not continue after ten o'clock'. Fines of one shilling were soon to be imposed on any member who neglected to open the debate assigned to him (unless he provide a substitute). And 'any member who is not present at the time appointed for the meeting shall be fined sixpence and, if he be absent the whole evening, an additional sixpence except he be unavoidably absent'. This rather cumbersome wording indicates concern about the possible non-appearance of a speaker leading for the affirmative or negative causing problems: the quick phone call was not, of course, an option then.

At the next meeting, the law referring to the fining of speakers who fail to appear at the appointed hour was repealed. Fines were not the sort of thing one would expect in a society of business and professional men. The meeting also resolved that a subject for debate could not be put forward by anyone wishing to lead in the affirmative until he had found another member prepared to speak in the negative.

With a rotating chairmanship in the first few meetings of the Edgbaston society, no particular prestige attached to being in the chair. There never was an office of chairman and where one is referred to, it is only to the man in the chair at that particular moment. At the first meeting for example, John Barlow, who was in the chair at the time, was elected secretary. He was one of the prime movers in the new society. Alfred Louis was elected treasurer at the same time and both appointments were for the ensuing year only. The secretary was instructed to purchase a minute book and to enter the minutes of this first meeting. He was also instructed to ask the Birmingham & Edgbaston Proprietary School if its library could be used for further meetings. The society was named the Edgbaston Debating Society and then Barlow vacated the chair to allow the meeting, now chaired by Alfred Louis, to pass a vote of thanks for 'his able and impartial conduct in the chair'.

The second meeting of the society was held only eleven days later on 19th October 1846. This time Edward Peyton was in the chair and this, as he was only third in the queue, suggests that neither Henry Greenhow nor Herbert Wright were present. The meeting was faced with an immediate problem. A Mr Partridge had written a letter on behalf of the committee of the school agreeing to the society using its library. However, there were conditions imposed by the school and precisely what they were is not clear from the minutes of the meeting. The secretary was asked to reply as tactfully as possible that the terms could not be accepted and to ask whether the reason for wanting the room could be explained on some other ground. It is difficult to draw conclusions from this. It could have been, for example, that the school was concerned about the possible subject matter of the debates. As already explained, this was an age in which any criticism of authority could be interpreted as seditious. Is it possible that the school feared that the society was potentially a hotbed of dangerous radicals? At this time most schools were run by the Church of England, which was firmly part of the establishment, and there was no national education system. In fact, the first debate of the society in three weeks time was to be on that very issue.

The society met again, for the third time, at the Plough & Harrow Hotel in Hagley Road, Edgbaston, on 12th November 1846. Henry Greenhow was in the chair this time. As he was first in the original ballot, but unavoidably absent at the previous meeting, it seems that he or others in a similar situation did not lose their place in the queue. In the twentieth century, the Plough & Harrow was Edgbaston's most reputed hostelry, as it still is today, and it can be assumed that it was so in the nineteenth as well. It was run in 1846 by a Mr and Mrs Dee and the secretary was asked to negotiate the use of a room on 'such terms as he might think best'. The meeting began with the election of some new members and the consideration of a further letter from Mr Partridge of the Birmingham & Edgbaston Proprietary School which, it was resolved, should be minuted - but for some reason it wasn't. This leaves the reader with a loose end that remains unexplained to this day. The society never met at the school again.

The meeting then moved to its first debate on the motion that 'Is there any necessity for the establishment by Government of a system of national education?' Speaking in the affirmative was Herbert Wright and in the negative John Barlow. Only four other members spoke and, after the chairman had summed up, the votes were ten in favour and five against. Henry Greenhow left the chair and this allowed James Collins to take it for the sole purpose of proposing a vote of thanks to him. A fortnight later, the society met with Herbert Wright in the chair. Apart from dealing with routine matters such as the admission of new members, the society adopted the procedure of agreeing on the subject of the next debate, and the names of the two main speakers, before beginning the current evening's debate. In this case, the motion asked the question whether the crusades had been on the whole beneficial to mankind. Edward Peyton spoke in the affirmative and Alfred Louis in the negative. Seven other members contributed and the vote was ten to eight in favour of the motion. The evening concluded with the same procedure of the chairman vacating the chair so that a vote of thanks could be passed.

The society met again in December at the Plough & Harrow under the chairmanship of Edward Peyton. As only two weeks had passed since the last meeting, this suggests a commendable level of enthusiasm for the activities of the recently formed society. To understand this better, readers must take themselves back to 1846. Those attending the debates, which normally began at 7.30pm, would have already dined with their wives or with each other. The latter possibly offered a more interesting conversational prospect than the former! Nonetheless, they had to turn out on dark and often dank November evenings by foot, on horseback, or in their own carriages through streets and roads of Edgbaston that were lit by gas lamps, moderately by today's standards, or not lit at all. Some members of the society would have been driven to the meetings by their own or their fathers' coachmen. The latter would either have waited until the debate was over or would have returned at an agreed hour. Those waiting, usually because their journey from and to home was longer, would have passed the intervening time in a nearby tavern - somewhere cheaper and rougher than the Plough & Harrow. The debates would have taken place in a room lit by candles or paraffin lamps.

After having decided to move the date of the next meeting two weeks hence to 23rd December instead of Christmas Eve, the meeting debated whether the character of Napoleon was deserving of condemnation. Benjamin Matthews spoke in the affirmative and John Clark in the negative. Seven other members out of the 18 present made their contributions to the debate and, at 10.15pm, the debate was not wound up, but was deemed to be unfinished and accordingly adjourned to the next meeting. Holding a meeting so close to Christmas might not have been popular. The meeting was not well attended and, after the adjourned debate had continued to its conclusion in the New Year, the motion condemning Napoleon was carried by six votes to three with two abstentions.

These early motions suggest that the society law relating to subjects for debate was being carefully observed. Debates about the crusades and the character of Napoleon engaged the intellect, but could hardly be claimed to deal with contemporary issues. However, it should be remembered that Napoleon had died only 25 years previously. His remains had been brought back from St Helena to Les Invalides, Paris, only six years before the debating society was formed - a concession by the British to the French that was not without controversy.

The Edgbaston society's law that required avoidance of subjects of a theological character is more understandable if one recalls life as it was in 1846. Charles Darwin (1809-1882) had not yet published *The Origins of the Species by Means of Natural Selection* and was not to do so for another 13 years, and those who believed the Bible to be literal truth were in the majority. Roman Catholics had been emancipated only 17 years earlier, a decision by Parliament that was probably regarded by most of the populace as altogether too enlightened. Roman Catholics were regarded with considerable suspicion by low-church Anglicans and Nonconformists and, in their minds, the problems of the supposedly feckless Irish were linked to their adherence to Rome. The number of Roman Catholics in Birmingham, boosted by immigration, was well above the national average. John Henry Newman (1801-1890), leader of the Anglican Tractarian (or Oxford)

Movement, had converted to Roman Catholicism a year before the debating society was formed. He established the Birmingham Oratory and became a cardinal in 1879. In 1850, the Pope set up a network of territorial bishoprics in England - of which Birmingham was one - and this further offended the strongly Protestant nation. However, many realised that literal belief in religion, including heaven and hell, was the glue that held society together and was not something to be trifled with. It is said that Darwin postponed publishing *Origins* for so long for just this reason.

If the attendance on 23rd December was disappointing, the eight members present on 17th January 1847, the second meeting in the new year, were not enough (being less than two-fifths of the membership) to form a quorum. No business could be transacted but a debate did take place on a motion whether the execution of King Charles I was unjustifiable. It was difficult to understand from the minutes why this debate was not brought to a conclusion. The motion was, in fact, to be carried by a narrow margin of nine votes to eight at the next meeting in February. However, at that meeting, one of the Martineau brothers gave notice that he wished to propose a number of changes to the laws of the society. The original laws required the secretary to stand for annual election. Now all officers were to be required to do so. He also wanted the ballot, which decided the order in which chairmen were instated for one meeting, abolished. The officers of the society would henceforth be the president, two vice-presidents, a secretary and a treasurer. The president would chair all meetings and only in his absence would one of the vice-presidents substitute for him. All these changes were carried at a later meeting in the same month. They created the sort of arrangement one would normally expect in a modern debating society. The rather idealistic notion of rotating the chairmanship of meetings meant that everyone had a turn, but some would have been better at it than others. A few might have preferred to avoid the limelight. The meeting went on to elect Francis Owen Clark as president and William Elliott and Edward Peyton were elected as vice-presidents. Effectively, this made Clark the first president of the Edgbaston Debating Society.

In these early days, most motions were drafted in the form of a question. For example: 'Is the character of Oliver Cromwell deserving of admiration?' which was carried by nine votes to four and 'Was Socrates right in declining to escape from prison?' For some reason, no result of the latter debate was recorded. The founder members of the society clearly knew their history better than many of those who came after them. From now on the need to amend the laws of the society appeared to have run its course and the minutes focus on the frequent debates. For example 'Is a limited monarchy better suited for the welfare of the nation than a republic?' was defeated by eight votes to five. If this result seems surprising, one has to remember that - with no mass-circulation daily newspapers then - Queen Victoria was unknown, except in name only, by the general populace. Being unknown, Victoria was not popular in the sense that Queen Elizabeth II is popular today and, until the last decade of her long reign, she was often unpopular.

Another typical motion was 'Have dramatic representations, as they at present exist, an immoral tendency?' This was carried by eight votes to five. The motion was somewhat clumsily worded and the fact that it was supported is perhaps an indication of a growing pomposity and a desire to censor. There was little evidence that mid-Victorian theatre was lampooning the establishment generally or politicians and other society leaders in particular. There has always been a puritan disapproval of the theatre and the Victorians were reverting to Puritanism, or at least the appearance of it, after the licentious period of the Regency. The motion for next debate was 'Is capital punishment unnecessary in the present state of society in England?' which was carried by nine votes to three. Soon afterwards, the society considered 'Has the advent of Mohamet *(sic)* been on the whole beneficial to mankind?' which was carried by seven votes to four. The results of these debates give some clues as to the political attitudes of the members of the society. A Liberal - almost Radical - tinge is not difficult to detect. Support for Oliver Cromwell and a republican form of government, and for the abolition of capital punishment, would not have been forthcoming from a debating society in which rural Tory squires were predominant.

In May 1847 the society debated whether the changes in the laws on public education met with its approbation. It was decided that they did by seven votes to five. Before that, however, the society discussed a matter that Thomas Martineau had, at the previous meeting, given notice that he intended to raise: that the society adjourned until October and that the next meeting should consider business only - in other words, an annual general meeting would be held. What is interesting about this is that debates would effectively cease in the summer months. The pattern of holding an annual general meeting in Autumn primarily to elect officers of the society, and ending the session in the Spring, was one that has been followed by the society ever since. Clearly debates were intended to keep the winter warm and not to disturb tranquil Summer evenings.

There was nothing exceptional about the AGM of the Edgbaston society in October 1847. Some accounts were presented and accepted. Alfred Wills was prevailed upon to be honorary secretary and Clark became treasurer when he yielded the presidency. Thomas Martineau became the second president of the society for the 1847-48 session and was to serve in the office again in 1851-52. There was an amendment to the laws that took from the chair the right to sum up the arguments of both sides. It is just possible to conclude that these summings-up might have been tendentious at times. As explained earlier in this narrative, from this time until well into the next century, only the leading speaker in the affirmative had the right to sum up at the end of a debate.

The society met again two weeks later and decided that, in future, it would prefer to meet on Wednesdays rather than Thursdays. Notice was given that changes to the laws would be proposed at the next meeting. The proper procedures were thus being respected in that members were forewarned when a constitutional change was contemplated. In this case, it was proposed that the law that required a quorum of two-fifths of the membership to transact business should be abolished. With attendances of around ten or so, a quorum might be difficult to achieve on all occasions. An amendment led to the society agreeing to a quorum of 'one fourth' of the membership. The law that required debates to end at ten o'clock in the evening was amended to read 'half past ten'. It is difficult to understand why such a trivial matter should have been the subject of a law in the society's constitution.

The subjects chosen for debate in this period were challengingly intellectual. The contrasting characters of Macbeth and Lady Macbeth were discussed, as too were the merits of Queen Mary I. Eventually, one of the biggest issues of the day was debated: whether the present sad condition of Ireland was to be blamed on England's misgovernment? The motion was defeated by five votes to two. The merits of direct and indirect taxation were also debated, as was whether co-operation was better than competition. All these subjects for debate were chosen a meeting or two in advance. The law that provided for the order of rotation of chairmen of debates to be selected by ballot was repealed. It was beginning to be recognised that the original laws needed revision. This was understandable as things never turn out as expected and the first rules of any organisation or game need to be changed almost inevitably. The subjects for debate continued to be historical and political, including consideration of The Earl of Shaftesbury's Factory Acts. A motion in favour of universal suffrage was rejected by seven votes to one. Over 80 years were to pass before Great Britain became a universal democracy. It was not something the Victorian 'haves' would have wanted.

CHAPTER 4

The overthrow of the Orleanist monarchy in France in 1848 was the signal for revolutionary movements elsewhere in Europe. Metternich escaped from Austria to England. The Habeas Corpus Act was suspended in Ireland and Smith O'Brien was transported for attempting an insurrection. Extremists were beginning to dominate the Chartist movement. The Great Exhibition opened in May 1851. Lord Derby became prime minister in a short-lived Conservative ministry in 1852. In the same year in France, Louis Napoleon was proclaimed Emperor Napoleon III. The Crimean War began in March 1854.

In March 1848 John Barlow was censured for not attending a debate at which he was the opening speaker. What punishment was meted out is not explained in the minutes. The failure of one of the main speakers to put in an appearance is always disruptive and, in those pre-telephone days, it would have been altogether more difficult to re-organise matters or to find a late substitute. The Barlow situation led to agreement that an opening speaker could exchange his place in the queue with the chosen proposer of the motion for debate at the next meeting.

At the AGM in October 1848 Herbert Wright became president of the Edgbaston society. The secretary Edward Peyton gave his report which mentioned particularly that the average attendance was eleven members. The treasurer announced a surplus of four shillings and ten pence (equivalent to about £40 today), but one subscription of five shillings had not been paid. At the next meeting it was decided that the laws and a list of members should be printed. In January a law was changed in order to allow members to speak twice in a debate provided that the chairman allowed it. This was amended with the words 'until every member desirous of speaking has done so'. In April it was resolved that the president be requested to deliver an address to the society or, if unable to do so, one of the vice-presidents would take his place. This practice of the president of the society delivering a valedictory address became a feature of all annual general meetings until it petered out with the crisis of survival which the society was to face in the 1970s.

Another year passed and, at the 1849 AGM, Algernon Clark was elected president to succeed Herbert Wright. The secretary gave a lengthier report than he had previously. He pointed out that 15 new members had been elected since the previous AGM. A very few had resigned since the society was founded. The average attendance had remained about eleven, but it had gone from nine to 13 as the year progressed. The secretary alluded to the nature of the motions for debate which were becoming more political and contemporary. Debates about Socrates or the relative merits of King Charles I and II were all very well as long as members knew something about them. However, it seems certain that more history was taught in those days than today. The secretary's report also expressed a concern that debates were being dominated by a few members who, reading between the lines, were clearly star performers given to hogging the limelight. He went on to suggest that, once the subject of future debates were known, members should do their homework so that they had something to contribute.

Algernon Clark yielded the presidency in the first meeting of the 1850-51 session and was presented with an address and three books: *The Works of William Hazlitt,* Lander's *Imaginary Conversations* and Blanchard's *Sketches from Life*. Vice-president Edward Taylor was elected in his place. A few weeks later, the society was debating whether the doctrines of phrenology were founded on truth and reason. Robert Francis Martineau, only 20 years old, led in the affirmative on this somewhat esoteric motion. Other subjects for debate at this time on Shakespearean and historical subjects also add to the impression that the leading speakers particularly were showing off their knowledge. Any member proposing a motion for debate took next place in the queue, and it appears that neither the officers nor a committee (which in the early days didn't exist) were involved in a process of selection. However, a committee of four headed by the president Edward Taylor was appointed for the first time in May 1850. Previously, the laws of the society stated that, for the purposes of the transaction of business, the entire membership present was a committee.

Alfred Wills made more than one attempt to introduce a change to the laws in order to re-introduce fines for a proposer or opposer who arrived late - that is after 8.00pm. Wills wanted a half-crown fine, by no means a negligible sum (equivalent to £25 today). Robert Francis Martineau suggested that the time be altered to 7.30pm. It was all to be of no avail as the proposed change was to be rejected by a substantial majority. At a meeting later in the year, another member tried to put back the starting time of debates to 8.20pm. This was withdrawn because of lack of support. The author is, of course, using the modern way of expressing time. In those days, it would typically have been spoken and written as 'eight o'clock (or twenty minutes past eight) in the evening'.

At a meeting of the Edgbaston society in November 1850, John Michell, the vice-president who was in the chair, drew attention to an advertisement which had appeared in The *Birmingham Journal* about the formation of another debating society which would meet at the Philosophical Rooms. The advertisement claimed that no debating society in the area existed and it was thought it necessary to contradict this. It was agreed that the secretary should write to the editor pointing out his error. Whilst communications in the mid-nineteenth were nothing like today's, and Edgbaston was a less integrated part of Birmingham than it became a generation or two later, it is slightly surprising that the advertiser was unaware of the society in Edgbaston. Although the minutes on the matter don't make it clear, one can assume that the proposed society was to be the second Birmingham Debating Society, founded on 26th November 1850, after the first one had collapsed a few months earlier.

Comment was also made on the scanty attendance at the Edgbaston society's meetings and it was agreed that members should call on the habitual absentees to persuade them to support the society better. In 1851 some more constitutional tinkering went on. The required quorum for business was changed from one fourth of the membership to eight members and another law was altered so that the five officers and five members would form a committee.

Robert Francis Martineau served as vice-president but, when the secretary Robert Coad resigned, he was elected to fulfil that role. He was replaced as vice-president by a relatively new member, William Izod. Maxwell Blews, who joined the society in 1849, complained in a letter about the way the minutes were written. This led to Blews suffering the indignity of a vote of censure and it took the casting vote of William Izod, who was in the chair, to save him. Frustratingly, there is nothing in the minutes which makes it clear what the dispute was about. Perhaps to criticise an officer of the society in any way was not the 'done thing'. It can't have been too serious as Blews became a vice-president later in the year.

John Michell, in his capacity as vice-president, occupied the chair several times. This appears to be because Algernon Clark, who was elected president in 1849, was not able to attend meetings presumably because of ill health or for some other unexplained reason. He retired in January 1850 after four months in office and Edward Taylor then completed his term for him. The debates were attracting only a dozen or so members, but a members' supper was held for the first time.

At the AGM in April 1851 it was proposed that the society should look for a room in 'the town' for meetings. The town being referred to was

Birmingham, and the Plough & Harrow in Edgbaston was considered to be inconveniently on the outskirts. Eventually the committee settled on the Hen & Chickens Hotel in New Street and it became the regular meeting place. After earlier meetings at the Philosophical Institution in Cannon Street, the same hostelry was being used by the Birmingham Debating Society and the momentum building up to the eventual merger four years later, with hindsight, appears inexorable. The fact that Birmingham was where the members worked rather than lived was the main reason for the move: they came to meetings direct from the office after taking supper *en route*. At this time, partners and managers worked long hours, like the people they employed.

The problems the society faced might also in part have had something to do with the motions chosen for debate. For example, the last subject debated in this season was whether Cardinal Wolsey was more activated by love of his religion than selfishly ambitious motives. Whilst this is the sort of subject that students of history would enjoy, it is difficult one for those who are not. Nonetheless, the secretary in his report reminded members of the objective of the society to cultivate powers of speaking and thinking. And, he might have added, that if members didn't know much about Cardinal Wolsey, they should have taken the trouble to learn.

Eventually, the almost inevitable happened and, at a meeting in December, there were insufficient members in attendance to form a quorum. Proceedings were suspended and it was agreed to re-convene a week later. The blame should not fall on the choice of motion, but on the trouble it took in that era to travel anywhere in a horse-drawn conveyance on cold winter evenings. The starting time for debates was constantly being altered from 7.30pm to 8.00pm and back again. The attendance tended to rise a little as Spring approached, but there were not, of course, meetings during the Summer.

The secretary Charles Mathews reported that, during 1852, there were four debates on historical subjects, three on political issues, two on literary matters and three on social issues. The average number attending debates was 13. The secretary emphasised the responsibility of everyone in the society to invite guests and introduce new members. Mathews was involved in local schools - particularly the King Edward VI Grammar School - and education policy. He was ideally suited to be a meticulous honorary secretary of the society.

In spite of the low level of support in the previous year, the AGM in October 1852 was well attended. This marked the beginning of the seventh session in the life of the society. Thomas Martineau, the outgoing president, was in the chair and gave a valedictory speech after a dinner. Samuel Timmins, a businessman who later was to do much for Birmingham, was elected president to succeed Martineau. The two men, and several others in the society, played a major part in the development and work of the National Education League twenty years later. Many long-term political relationships were forged in the early days of the society.

A meeting two weeks later at the Hen & Chickens was chaired by the vice-president, William Hudson. This was because the president, Samuel Timmins, was going to lead for the negative in the scheduled debate on whether a limited monarchy was a better form of government than a republic. Timmins was also allowed to speak from the floor in order to propose an amalgamation with the Birmingham Debating Society. This was seconded by the secretary, Charles Mathews. Thomas Martineau said that the Birmingham society had sent him a number of tickets to its next debate in order to allow Edgbaston members to witness how Birmingham went about things. For an unexplained reason, this minute was later deleted. Edward Martineau proposed that discussion of the matter be deferred to the next meeting and this was carried only narrowly by eight votes to six. Two weeks later, the society met again and decided to reject politely the overtures from the Birmingham Debating Society. It is possible that the professional young men of Edgbaston regarded themselves as a cut above the Birmingham manufacturers who were reportedly a little older, but the realities of the situation were to become pressing. Subsequent meetings lowered the quorum necessary to deal with business and it was eventually reduced to six.

Almost from 1846 onwards there were those who were members of both the Birmingham and Edgbaston societies and, consequently, the idea of an amalgamation was soon being discussed inside and outside meetings. It was to happen eventually in 1855 after the first Birmingham society had ceased to function in 1850 and the new one had been formed to replace it later in the same year. There is little in the records to explain why the first society was closed down, but lack of support might have been the reason. However, that makes it difficult to understand why a second Birmingham society was formed so soon afterwards, with many of the same personalities involved, and was able to survive until the eventual amalgamation with the Edgbaston society. It is possible that some members of the first Birmingham society thought that it was being run in a rather too informal way compared to the Edgbaston society. John Winfield, the honorary secretary and treasurer did join the second Birmingham society, but only remained a member for a few months. Perhaps he had lost interest. Another interesting clue to the relationship between the first and second Birmingham societies is an 1852 minute stating that there had been a gentleman's agreement that the first Birmingham society should hand over its cash surplus to the second. The minute referred to the fact that this agreement had not yet been fulfilled and the secretary was asked to do something about it.

The so-called Committee of Questions of the first Birmingham society became, in 1851, the Committee for the Session comprising six members and the secretary. There were frequent references to chairmen in the records, particularly in those of the first society, but these were chairmen of meetings. The office as such did not exist. The chairman of meetings came to be referred to as presidents, but everyone took a turn to preside over one debate. The second Birmingham society properly elected presidents from the outset, the first being James Timmins Chance. George Jabet was honorary secretary of the second society during its first two years of life. He then succeeded Chance as president.

The meeting place of the Birmingham society was the Hen & Chickens public house in New Street. George Dixon spoke in a number of debates and he was to become president in 1854. In the fullness of time he was to become an MP and an exceptional public servant. There was a secret ballot for the office of president in 1854 in which it appears that all members were considered to be candidates whether they wished it or not. When Robert Wright was given the most votes, he declined to accept office and another ballot was required. This time, George Dixon was chosen. If that wasn't enough, the ballot for secretary produced a tie between John Turner and Henry Howell. The latter solved the problem by withdrawing.

The Birmingham society had other 'moments'. One was in 1853 when Clement Mansfield Ingleby, a future chairman of the amalgamated society, was too ill to lead in a debate, so he sent in a written paper instead. The society also managed to raise £25 by subscription from members to support the building fund of the new Birmingham and Midland Institute, even if this fell short of the target of £50. Although attendances were generally modest, a public debate organised by the society at the Philosophical Institution in January 1853 attracted an attendance of 200. The subject discussed was whether Louis Napoleon's Second Empire would be beneficial to France.

From October 1852 onwards the possibility of amalgamation with the Edgbaston society was discussed with increasing frequency. There is no doubt that the Birmingham society wanted and needed the amalgamation.

The demise of the first Birmingham society and the lack of detailed records of both it and the second society has made it inevitable, as pointed out at the beginning of this narrative, that the story of the Birmingham & Edgbaston Debating Society in its early days is predominantly the story of the Edgbaston society.

Maxwell Blews was a leading speaker in an Edgbaston society debate in 1852 and failed to put in an appearance. He also failed to provide an excuse in writing and was fined two shillings. Thomas Watts did the same thing a year later, but his apology was considered to be sufficiently abject and he was not fined. In fact, he became president in 1854. This was the second incident involving Blews and perhaps he was difficult. Early in 1853 a member called Edward Keep resigned as he was about to emigrate to Australia. In the mid-nineteenth century, one can only reflect on the enterprise that this course of action involved.

One of the Edgbaston society debates in 1853 was on the desirability of a large extension to the franchise. As this was still 14 years before the Second Reform Bill, it suggests that the society was thinking ahead of its time. A few weeks later there was a motion to abolish capital punishment. It was defeated by the relatively narrow margin of 13 votes to nine. Only two decades earlier there were over 200 offences for which somebody could be hanged, including minor crimes such as poaching.

In May 1853 it was decided that the last meeting of the present session in the following month should be of a 'fuller character' than the ordinary meetings of the society and be open to the public. It was suggested that the meeting should be held in the theatre of the Philosophical Institution. A sub-committee was appointed to make the arrangements. The subject for debate chosen was that the present condition of Ireland is mainly attributable to misgovernment by England. This was to be advertised in the *Midland Counties Herald* and the *Birmingham Journal*. The sub-committee suggested that no routine business matters be discussed and that the debate should begin as soon as the chair was taken.

When the day came, the members turned out in good numbers as did a number of others, to form what the minutes described as a 'large and highly respectable audience of ladies and gentlemen'. Three speakers, rather than the usual two, were lined up for both the affirmative and negative. Samuel Timmins, the president, was in the chair and Thomas Martineau opened the debate. William Mathews led for the negative. The motion was carried by 13 votes to 12 with six abstentions. When one considers that over one million Irish died of starvation and another million emigrated in the famine years from 1846 to 1848, Britain could hardly deny some responsibility. Nonetheless, there was a tendency for the British to blame what they believed to be the feckless Catholic Irish themselves for their troubles and it comes as no great surprise that a cross-section of Birmingham business and professional men should be evenly divided.

Thomas Martineau sought, at this time, to abolish the office of vice-president. This involved a minor change to the constitution, removing any reference to vice-presidents. This also affected the law that one of the vice-presidents would take the chair if the president was absent. From hereon, if the president was absent, the chairman of the meeting would be elected by those present. Thomas Martineau, by now a young lawyer, comes across from the records as one of the stronger personalities in the nascent society. He had clearly recognisable leadership qualities which were to be proven by his subsequent achievements in both his commercial career and public service. In 1852, at the age of 24, he had by now entered into partnership with Arthur Ryland and one of Birmingham's most eminent legal practices was in the making. Two decades later, another member of the Edgbaston Debating Society, John Barham Carslake, was to join the partnership in 1874 and his family, like the Martineaus, was to provide several partners in the hundred years which followed. Arthur Ryland never joined the society, but some members of his family did. However, he was Mayor of Birmingham 1860-61 and a long-serving secretary and then a president of the Birmingham Law Society.

In October 1853 the society opened the new session with a *conversazione* (an Italian word that normally describes a social gathering for the purpose of discussion about a literary or arts-related subject) and the annual general meeting. The president, Samuel Timmins, was in the chair. The secretary, Charles Mathews, gave his report, telling those present that there were 66 members. However, the largest attendance in the session which ended in the Spring was 40 and the smallest had been 13. He had worked out that average attendance had been 23. Whilst these figures were the best so far in the society's history, the secretary was clearly anxious about the future and appealed for a higher level of support from the membership. Another letter was received at this time from the Birmingham Debating Society suggesting a joint social meeting. This led to the appointment of yet another sub-committee to examine the amalgamation proposal. The result was a meeting of representatives of both societies at the New Inn, Handsworth.

Some rule changes were made and it appears that, whilst Thomas Martineau had not succeeded in abolishing the office of vice-president, the society had agreed on one incumbent rather than two. Thomas Watts was chosen for the office immediately after William Mathews had been elected president. Watts was to succeed him a year later. The newly elected committee was asked to look at the laws of the society and its proposals were adopted in November. In January 1854 the society debated whether Byron should be considered a 'poet of high order'. The motion was defeated by 11 votes to three with seven abstentions. This sort of motion reflects well on the learning of the society and it is almost impossible to contemplate the society debating a motion of this type today. The same might be said of the next two historical subjects debated: 'that the revolution of 1688 was unjustifiable and inglorious' and 'that the character of Archbishop Cranmer was not such as to entitle him to the reputation of a great reformer'.

In April 1854 another joint debate with the Birmingham society had to be postponed because there was no agreement about a motion. At the *conversazione* following the last debate of the session, the secretary reported that the largest number attending a debate had been 37 and the smallest 20. In April 1855 the society debated the system of promotion in the British army. The Crimean War had brought the issue of purchase of commissions to the fore, but it was to be another 15 years before the Cardwell army reforms were introduced. The last debate of the session was organised jointly with the Birmingham society. The subject was the reconstitution of Poland and the secretary reported in the minutes of 'a numerous and highly respectable audience of ladies and gentlemen'.

CHAPTER 5

Lord Palmerston became prime minister in 1855. The Indian Mutiny began in March 1857 and the Massacre of Cawnpore took place in June. The War of Italian Liberation began in 1859 and the Civil War in North America started in 1860.

The *conversazione* and AGM at the start of the new session in October 1855 brought to the fore an increasing desire amongst members to amalgamate with the Birmingham society. Motions were passed which effectively asked the committee to assess feeling on the matter. This led to the committee recommending at the next meeting that the two societies should amalgamate and this, proposed by Thomas Martineau and seconded by Samuel Timmins, was carried. The latter was a consistent advocate of a merger for several years. As mentioned earlier, very few records of the Birmingham Debating Society are in existence apart from a register of members and it seems clear that in every discernible way, membership and number of meetings per annum for example, the Edgbaston society was dominant. It could allow itself to defer to the larger town, if not the larger society, and accept the name Birmingham & Edgbaston Debating Society. In the minutes of the first meeting of the new society, the secretary John Green omitted 'Birmingham' from the title and had to insert it afterwards!

The election of Edgbaston Debating Society officers for 1855-56 had already gone ahead at the October AGM and Henry Chance had been elected president and Clement Mansfield Ingleby vice-president. As it happened, these two men had a foot in both camps and this may in part explain why they were accepted, without dissent from the Birmingham members, as the first two occupants of the same offices in the amalgamated society. In fact the Birmingham society had only asked to be allowed to nominate two members of the first committee. Consequently the rules were changed to allow a committee of five (apart from the officers) instead of three and it is noticeable that it was the Edgbaston society's rules that were changed. Henry Chance was one of three members of his family in the Birmingham society's list. Chance Brothers & Company became the largest makers in Britain of window glass, plate glass, lighthouse lenses and optical glass. Another famous firm in the local glass trade was Osler & Company.

Several members of the Osler family joined the society during the next 100 years and two were to serve as president.

After the first Birmingham Debating Society had been dissolved in 1850, the second society, with the same name, had been formed on 26th November 1850 and lived on until the merger on 14th November 1855. The first society, which had a lower age limit of 18, recruited only about 30 members in its four years of existence and the second less than 100 in total. About 180 gentlemen joined the Edgbaston society between 1846 and 1855, but quite a number of them had resigned two or three years after they had joined. It was inevitable that the amalgamation caused some members to reconsider their attachment to the combined society and it is difficult to know whether some sort of re-affirmation was required. Generally, the level of attendance at any one time represented a low proportion of the members on the books. The first Birmingham society was dissolved because of lack of support and the second society might not have survived had the amalgamation not taken place. Its secretary, William Allen, had written to its members in 1854 complaining about lax attendance. At one meeting in that year, for example, only the two opening speakers attended. They were understandably annoyed about the situation and the debate was aborted.

Both societies would have known of the existence of the other almost from the outset and the fact that they co-existed rather than coalesced into a single society was entirely because of geography. But, as already mentioned, this had very quickly ceased to matter as the majority of Edgbaston society members were, in effect, commuters who would not have had the time to call in at their homes before setting out again to attend meetings held in the centre of Birmingham (at the Hen & Chickens). But in the end, the logic of an amalgamation could hardly be resisted.

An extract from the Edgbaston society's minute book stated that: 'Accordingly on the 14th November 1855 the two societies became one under the name of the Birmingham and Edgbaston Debating Society. In conclusion your Committee trust that the two societies having become one, may flourish within the precincts of their native Town; that the same courtesy and good feeling which distinguishes each, may be yet more eminent in the two united and that the Birmingham and Edgbaston Debating Society may enjoy prolonged prosperity and become an ornament to the Town, adding one more proof to the old adage - UNITY IS STRENGTH.' The Victorians were given, on such occasions, to signing off with this sort of over-effusive valediction.

The first meeting of the combined society took place on 12th December 1855 at the Hen & Chickens Hotel. It reviewed the rules which, as has been pointed out, were already very similar and what emerged did not much differ from those of the Edgbaston society. The minutes continued to be recorded in the Edgbaston book. Any reader of club and society minutes taken in the Victorian era cannot fail to notice the punctiliousness of the typical committee's behaviour. It 'begs to recommend' and understands that it is the servant of the membership. Members then would not put up with anything amounting to arrogance and a disregard for correct procedure.

One innovation of the Birmingham society from 1851 onwards was for the secretary to send out to members a large selection of subjects for debate, sometimes as many as 40, inviting them to volunteer on which they would like to lead in the affirmative or negative. This was to be continued for a number of years after the merger. Amongst the first motions debated by the amalgamated society, in January 1856, was on slavery in the USA. The abolitionist cause won narrowly by six votes to four. This was still four years before the American Civil War started.

38 members attended a meeting in March 1856 at which Charles Mathews resigned from committee and was replaced by Thomas Martineau. Mathews, a solicitor and a man of accomplishment and charm, was to return as president four years later. There were two other members of the Mathews family in the society, the already mentioned William and George, who also served as presidents. Soon afterwards, Henry Chance sent in his resignation as president by letter. It was not clear whether, by doing so, he was setting a precedent that the presidential term of office should be for a single annual session. If anything, the precedent had already been established by both societies. Clement Mansfield Ingleby, a solicitor who had recently been a secretary and treasurer of The Birmingham Law Society, was elected president to succeed Chance. A year later, in October 1857, 47 members attended the AGM. Cornelius T Saunders was elected president with the immediate past president Clement Mansfield Ingleby remaining on the committee. It was reported that the society now had 116 members and the average attendance was 23. The habit of keeping a check on average attendances continued for over 100 years. Throughout most of its history, only about 20 percent of society members could be described as 'active'.

The 18 year-old Joseph Chamberlain joined the Edgbaston society in November 1854 as soon as he had moved there from London to work in the family's business in Birmingham, Nettlefold & Chamberlain. He arrived virtually not knowing a soul, but somebody told him about the society. He was proposed for membership by Charles Mathews, who was to become one of his lifelong friends. Chamberlain took part in his first debate a fortnight later, speaking in defence of Oliver Cromwell. This motion was surprisingly lost by 15 votes. This is perhaps an indication of how political and historical fashion changes. Cromwell's reputation today stands very high indeed, but it was not always the case. A month later, Chamberlain spoke in favour of the French revolution. Chamberlain was to be nicknamed 'Radical Joe' when his political career started but, at this early stage of his life, his ideas were still taking shape. The long and impressive political career that was to follow was to be characterised by a rightward movement that led ultimately to a change of party.

The young Chamberlain also played an active part in a debate that 'the official career of Lord Palmerston does not entitle him to the character of a wise and honest statesman'. Chamberlain spoke in support of the motion, criticising the great man. The popular Palmerston was a Whig rather than a Liberal. Some would have considered him to be a Canningite Tory. At the Foreign Office, his policy was often cavalier and bellicose. This made him a popular hero with the masses, but perhaps less so with moderate opinion. Nonetheless, it was the Crimean War made him prime minister in 1855 in just the same way as war was to make Winston Churchill prime minister in 1940. The members of the debating society were probably more in tune with the Liberals and Palmerston's eventual heir, William Gladstone. In spite of Chamberlain's efforts in the society debate, the motion on Palmerston was lost by one vote.

In the 1857-58 session Chamberlain, now 21, began to attend debates regularly. The first record of him leading in a debate was when he proposed successfully (by 12 votes to eight) that Thackeray's writings were superior to those of Dickens. Chamberlain left early and could not sum up, so Charles Mathews undertook the task. This is hardly something that the society would have approved of but, with his boundless self-confidence, Chamberlain got away with it without censure. He was not yet a politician in the making and many years were to pass before he showed an inclination towards public life. Nonetheless, he spoke frequently in debates. He led for the negative against a change in the law of conspiracy, and in the affirmative that physical well-being is essential to intellectual and moral development. In both cases, he carried the day. He was soon to become secretary of the society.

Joseph Chamberlain came from a strict Unitarian family in London. He was to make his fortune from several manufacturing enterprises, particularly from screw manufacture. This latter business had been started by J S

Nettlefold with the support of Joseph Chamberlain's father who was also Nettlefold's brother-in-law. Nettlefold saw an American screw-making machine at The Great Exhibition in 1851 and, with the financial backing of Chamberlain senior, also called Joseph, he secured the English rights to it. When Joseph junior was sent from the comforts of London to Birmingham at the age of 18, it was to manage the commercial side of business. From the outset, he showed a great gift for salesmanship and one must presume that his father had already recognised his talents. He walked to the company's offices in Broad Street every morning at 9.00am from his rooms in Frederick Street and back again at 6.00pm, a distance of about 800 yards. He was to retire from business in early middle-age, having become very rich, in order to concentrate on public life. Three Chamberlain brothers joined the society: Arthur in 1858, Walter in 1863, who was to be honorary treasurer 1867-68 and became chairman of W.T. Avery, and Herbert in 1870 who was to be chairman of BSA. Another member, John Henry Chamberlain, was a local architect who was no relation to Joseph, but was patronised by him. Because he liked Berrow Court so much, Joseph Chamberlain asked him to build his home at Highbury. In all, eight members of the society in the nineteenth century were called Chamberlain, but whether others of them, apart from his son Neville, were blood relatives to Joseph is not known. The Chamberlains were far from uncultured. Joseph proposed a motion in April 1858 that the pre-Raphaelite element in modern art was founded on sound principles.

The first public debate, an idea conceived by the committee a year earlier, was held in January 1858 and 500 ladies and gentlemen attended. This was an impressive number that filled the New Theatre of the Midland Institute in Cannon Street, and was probably an all-time record attendance for the society. The subject debated, in the aftermath of the Indian Mutiny of course, was the future government of India.

Although the society did not meet to debate in the Summer, an annual outing was a regular feature of the programme at this time. The railway made these excursions possible and frequently 50 members or more would take part. These were day trips, so the chosen destinations were not too far away. Places visited included Worcester, Warwick, Evesham, Tewkesbury, Broadway, Bewdley, Kenilworth, Stratford upon Avon and Meriden. The day involved a bit of sightseeing and then dinner in a local hostelry followed by speeches that were, by all accounts, witty and erudite. Those taking part in these trips were transported, depending on the venue, either by rail or by four-horse omnibuses hired specially for the day. Eventually, the motor car and the freedom of travel it allowed, was to be a key factor in ending these group excursions. Nonetheless, in the years they occurred, they were well organised and the tickets which are preserved to this day include details of every train to be caught with precise timings.

Joseph Chamberlain became secretary of the society in 1859. According to Denis Judd, author of *Radical Joe: A Life of Joseph Chamberlain,* he developed, after an earlier tendency towards formal over-elaboration, into a self-assured and witty speaker. In his book *Joseph Chamberlain: Entrepreneur in Politics*, Peter Marsh tells us that it was 15 years before he could think on his feet. J L Garvin in his *Life of Joseph Chamberlain* wrote that it took years for Chamberlain to attain his succinct and lucid qualities of his mature speaking style. Like Judd, he also refers to the over-elaboration, even when Chamberlain was attempting humour. He adds that Chamberlain learnt his speeches by heart, but they 'reeked of the lamp'. His speeches were festooned with too may French quotations and they gave no hint of level of power he was eventually to attain in his public life.

In their biographies, both Marsh and Garvin recall a dinner party given by George Dixon in honour of John Bright. Chamberlain was there and Bright put forward his view that Gibraltar should be returned to the Spanish. Chamberlain did not treat the matter with the same lightness as the other guests and, ignoring Bright's pacifist principles, argued the case somewhat sneeringly and sarcastically. Bright reportedly enjoyed the argument, but it gives us an indication of Chamberlain's implacable character.

Chamberlain already wore the eyeglass that was to be his political trademark. During a society outing to Hagley ten years later, he proposed a toast to the 'artopsariacoluthic members' (the word refers to the followers of the loaves and fishes). He explained in a speech, punctuated by appreciative laughter and applause, that the members in question were those who always attended the annual dinner which was free, but never were seen at ordinary meetings. Very many years later, at the golden jubilee dinner in 1896, Chamberlain recalled that the society was a Liberal, almost Radical, body and that caused problems at the time with finding speakers to take the Tory line. Judd tells us that Chamberlain was more moderate than Radical when he was a member of the society. Also remembered at the jubilee dinner was the artopsariacoluthic speech by those who had heard it 27 years earlier and the local newspapers referred to it in their lengthy reports.

Joseph Chamberlain played a prominent part in the society's debate on John Bright in 1862. A motion for debate strongly condemned the principles enunciated by the Radical Member of Parliament, John Bright, in a speech in Birmingham, and 'the spirit in which they were delivered'. The speech was about a pacific foreign policy rather than domestic parliamentary reform, which was the burning issue at the time. Bright had been one of Manchester's Liberal MPs and had been unseated in 1857 because of his pacifist views. The electoral tide flowed strongly in favour of Palmerston in the aftermath of the Crimean War. Bright, a Quaker, was against the war and the policies adopted to suppress the Indian Mutiny and, as already mentioned, he favoured handing Gibraltar back to Spain. The Birmingham Liberals virtually gave him a parliamentary seat, as they were able to do with Tory opposition in the town being almost negligible, but he was expected to drop his opposition to the government's policy in India.

Bright had earlier made his name in his opposition, with Richard Cobden, to the Corn Laws. He was a great legislative reformer, but soft on foreign policy issues. This meant that he was the polar opposite to anti-reformist Palmerston. In those days parliamentary parties were much looser groupings than they are today. It was quite possible, with the limited enfranchisement of the population, for a party to win an election while some of its individual MPs lost their seats because of their personal positions on issues: disciplined parties and being 'on message' at all times were a long way into the future. Since the repeal of the Corn Laws, the Liberals had been a loose combination of Whigs like Palmerston, Peelite Tories including Gladstone, and Radicals such as Bright. The Tories had been split by the repeal of the Corn Laws and saw very little of power during the next thirty years.

Because of the importance of this debate, two nights were allotted to it. The theatre of the Midland Institute was the chosen venue. Chamberlain spoke against the motion and was again on the winning side. The vote (ten to nine) was surprisingly close and this suggested that Bright's views, particularly on parliamentary reform, had considerable support in the urban areas of the nation. The Imperial gospel, of which Chamberlain was eventually to be the high priest, had not taken hold of the British yet. Its high noon came at the end of the century when Chamberlain was Colonial Secretary.

Bright was opposed to Tory aristocratic control of the country and its institutions, which it was able to exercise in spite of the Liberal majority in the House of Commons. The second Reform Bill was still nearly ten years in the future and the nation was not in any sense fully democratic or near to being so. The great majority of the members of the debating society in this epoch would not have been Tories, but nor were they on the Radical fringe. They were middle-class - a section of society that represented a far smaller percentage of the total population than it does today. Some but not all of them would have been enfranchised by the first Reform Bill, so it is easy to understand their sympathy with the reformist policies of the Liberal party. As pointed out earlier, it was the Reform Bill of 1832 which gave Birmingham its first two MPs. Before that the city, or town as it then was, had no parliamentary representation at all. It would take the re-alignment of the parties in the next 50 years and the emergence of Labour to alter the political hue of the society and of Birmingham itself.

This debate on Bright had repercussions when the Rt Hon Charles Adderley MP, a junior minister, while addressing the House of Commons in a debate on reform, referred to the society. Quoting from his speech, Adderley said: 'With regard to the skilled artisans in Birmingham, no persons were more fit to enjoy the franchise. They have their debating clubs, and not long ago the question discussed at one of them was whether the honourable member (Bright) really represented them in this House. The result being that, in a vote, the honourable gentleman had a majority of one in his favour.'

To be referred to as 'skilled artisans' was too much for the committee and a letter was sent by the secretary, Charles Mathews, politely suggested to Adderley that he might be mistaken about the 'nature of the debating club' and explaining what the society was all about and the background of its members: university graduates, physicians, surgeons, architects, lawyers, manufacturers and tradesmen. He advised Adderley of the result and the names of the speakers for and against. This brought no more than a polite acknowledgement from Adderley's private secretary. It was proposed by Thomas Martineau and seconded by Chamberlain that correspondence with Adderley be recorded in the minute book.

By the standards of the time, the motion was strongly worded, but it seems immensely flattering that the vote of fewer than 20 gentlemen in a debate held in a provincial city should have attracted national attention. The situation does not, for example, appear to be in the same league as that of the Oxford Union 'king and country' debate in 1933. Unfortunately, it is difficult to draw conclusions because the record is frustratingly typical of all minutes of meetings. Minute takers are writing primarily for those present and assume that all those likely to read the record are already in the picture and only require an *aide memoire*. A more journalistic approach is needed to assist those who might, 150 years later, want to know what the issues were.

Joseph Chamberlain spoke in the debate to attack Bright's belief that non-intervention should be the touchstone of the nation's dealing with foreign states and that aristocracies were responsible for wars. Perhaps the process that led, a generation later, to Chamberlain changing parties (because of government policy towards Ireland) had its beginnings here. He was to become a Tory imperialist.

As a postscript to this matter, the correspondence between Mathews and Adderley, later Lord Norton, was eventually copied in 1921 to J L Garvin, a legendary editor of *The Observer* who was writing a life of Joseph Chamberlain and wanted to know something of the latter's association with the society. Adderley, as it happened, was an expert on local government and a very public-spirited man. He let what is now Adderley Park to the Corporation for a nominal rent and gave the Hams Hall estate to the people of Birmingham.

Another young man, John Thackray Bunce, was chosen as president for the 1858-59 session. He was to become a Freeman of the City of Birmingham in 1899. By that time, he had been an outstanding journalist and the editor of *The Birmingham Daily Post* (eventually *The Birmingham Post*) for forty years and was author of the first volumes of the *History of the Corporation* and also wrote *The History of King Edward's Foundation* and *Birmingham Life Sixty Years Ago* amongst what was a prolific output of historical works, including a biography of Josiah Mason.

The Hen & Chickens Hotel had remained the venue for all debates but, in January 1859, members were persuading the committee that the Birmingham & Midland Institute was more in keeping with the dignity of the society. The secretary was asked to find out whether the council of the institute would make available the Patent Specification Library. The institute agreed at a fee of a half guinea per evening. The entire correspondence was copied laboriously into the minute book. In the end, the Hen & Chickens continued to be used and it seems that the institute was reserved only for special occasions.

There was another motion in February 1859 that criticised armed intervention in the internal affairs of other countries, thus damning Palmerston's conduct of foreign policy. Chamberlain spoke against the motion and was once more on the winning side. Votes after debates at this time were affected by the fact that many members were leaving before they were concluded. Whatever the excuse, this was hardly good manners.

Chamberlain wrote to the Lord-Lieutenant of Warwickshire in 1859 urging him to allow the society to form a company of rifle volunteers from its members. The request was refused and Chamberlain wrote back stating that he had lost the services of a fine body of men. The society then formed its own non-official rifle corps. The Lord-Lieutenant's fear that armed groups of citizens with radical opinions might lead to insurrection was a typical Tory over-reaction in those times.

The issue of parliamentary reform and the franchise became an issue for all political groupings in the 1860s. A bill introduced by Lord John Russell was debated on the grounds that it was nothing more than a minimum expedient to check agitation on the subject. The society agreed that was just what it was, by 20 votes to nine. In the 1861-62 session many of the subjects debated by the society were political. Whether Chamberlain had something to do with this can only be guessed at. The committee report drew attention with satisfaction to a membership of 162. However, the average attendance at debates had dropped from 47 to 39. The meetings of the rifle corps, and the consequent martial ardour, was criticised on the grounds that it undermined the 'calm spirit of philosophical enquiry' in debates. The committee report also drew attention to the fact that poor attendance at society debates reflected what was happening in the House of Commons.

The Report of the Committee, beautifully written in Joseph Chamberlain's neat script, mentioned three members who had been expelled because of failure to pay their subscriptions. The report reflected on the motions and drew attention to the fact that there were more 'theoretical' motions than previously. As befits the aspiring politician, Chamberlain commented on the political issues debated and concluded with an appeal to the members to support the society.

George Dixon joined the amalgamated society in 1861. He had been a member of the second Birmingham Debating Society from the day it was formed and was its last president (1854-55). His subsequent record of public service was outstanding. He became a town councillor in 1864 and was mayor in 1866, MP for Birmingham 1867-76 and again for Edgbaston 1885-98. Unsurprisingly, he became a Freeman of the city in 1898.

The American Civil War had begun by this time and the society debated that 'the conduct of the Northern States in regard to the question of slavery has been disingenuous and that the best solution of the difficulty is to be expected from the accomplishments of the southern secession'. Only ten members turned up for the debate and Joseph Chamberlain proposed a two-week adjournment. This time only eight appeared and another adjournment was agreed. In the end, the motion was never debated, but others relating to the war were to be. It is interesting that the wording of some of these motions lent towards sympathy for the secessionist states and this reflected the prevailing attitudes of those on the right of the political spectrum at the time. The way of life in the Southern states was seen as more English and few regarded the war at that stage to be a crusade against slavery. Another debate on the war considered a motion that 'it has become the duty of the European governments to recognise the Southern Confederacy and to open the blockade of the southern ports'. Joseph Chamberlain spoke in support of the motion, but it was defeated by 19 votes to six. The blockade was debated again a few months later and this perhaps indicates a failure to grasp the realities of modern warfare. It is almost as if there was something not quite sporting about preventing supplies from reaching both sides. This time the motion was carried by ten votes to three.

CHAPTER 6

In 1863 the Prince of Wales married Princess Alexandra of Denmark. The next year, Britain declined to give help to Denmark over the Duchies of Schleswig and Holstein. The American Civil War ended in 1865, but President Lincoln was assassinated. In June 1866 war broke out between Prussia and Saxony. Austria supported Saxony and was defeated at Sadowa.

Joseph Chamberlain was elected president of the society for the 1862-63 session. He had by now become the dominant personality in the society, even though he was barely 30 years old. But his eyes were on further horizons and it was his successor, Sebastian Evans JP, who had to deal with flagging interest in debates. The latter proposed in February 1864 that the society be dissolved, stating that the meetings were not interesting enough. An amendment by John Thackray Bunce (president 1858-59) that the committee should consider ways of making meetings more 'attractive' was carried unanimously and Evans withdrew his motion. The committee now proposed that (1) debates should not be held at the Midland Institute unless the ventilation was improved, (2) the committee should be enlarged from five to nine, (3) there should be two public debates per session, (4) there should be three secretaries instead of one, and (5) tea and coffee should be provided at meetings. All these points were supported unanimously, except the last which was carried by the narrow margin of 17 votes to 14.

These proposals led to some sort of revival and a well-attended debate on a non-political subject, comparing the merits of Robert Browning to Alfred Tennyson, ended in favour of the latter by 40 votes to eleven. The numbers attending debates regularly rose into the forties and it makes one wonder if the egotistical Chamberlain had been more concerned with his own career and how the society might serve that end, rather than with the interests of the society itself.

The motions debated in this decade do provide clues as to what were the burning issues of the time. For example, a motion that trades, professions and clerkships should be open to women was defeated. Another motion proposed that the reform question could only be settled by universal suffrage and a plurality of votes attaching to property. This was just carried, but it is another indication that educated men of those times could not get their heads round the idea that ownership of property was not a good reason for an unspecified number of extra votes, or that women might be allowed to vote. It is unfortunate that only results of debates are recorded in the minutes of the time, and nothing of what had been said.

A motion in 1864 that Palmerston was not a great statesman was carried by nine votes to two. This was the second time a motion had been debated which attacked Palmerston and the margin was overwhelming this time. However, a very small attendance can lead to unexpected results. The vote appears either to be a 'Little Englander' condemnation of Palmerston's somewhat gung-ho foreign policy, or a prudish condemnation of the man's morals. The political colour of the society in its early years had been Cobdenite. The Liberal coalition still included Whigs, but the latter were a disappearing breed by now. The centre of gravity of the party was beginning to move leftwards, but the process was too slow to prevent the rise of Labour a generation later. The debating society, if the results of debates are anything to go by, did not move with this tide. By the last decade of the nineteenth century its verdicts in political debates would have won the approval of Lord Salisbury.

The Conservatives remained where they had always been after the Peelites had split away from the party in 1846. The were still the 'country' party and remained so until the politics of business and economics assumed much greater significance than hitherto. As already mentioned in this narrative, the terms *left* and *right* were not much used forms of political shorthand in that era. The idea that Palmerston, because he led the Liberal/Whig coalition, was anywhere near to being on the radical or left half of the political spectrum would have been considered laughable to his contemporaries.

Birmingham was still a Liberal city at this time and, until the mid-1860s, the hard-working professional men who were members of the society would have felt a greater affinity with Liberalism than with the rural squirearchy that was the backbone of the Tory party. This changed when Benjamin Disraeli broadened the appeal of the Tory party. Disraeli in his younger days never believed that only the House of Commons should be representative of the nation. For him, the monarchy and the aristocracy were also part of the structure of government and he believed that, without them, government would become middle-class despotism. Perhaps reluctantly, he came to accept the inevitable but had died before the Third Reform Bill of 1884 was passed.

For the present, the society was delivering verdicts in its debates of which Gladstone would have approved. However, in the last two decades of the nineteenth century, it became predominantly Tory. Nobody was more representative of this metamorphosis than Joseph Chamberlain himself who crossed the floor of the Commons in 1886, and Birmingham followed him.

The committee's report on the session 1865-66 stated that membership had been boosted by 45 new members and had risen to 195. It commented on the fact that the most poorly attended debate attracted only 18 and the 'semi-public' debate drew 157. The motion at the former concerned the Bank Charter Act and it is possible that the choice of subjects for debate was having an effect on attendances. Nonetheless, the average attendance was a not unimpressive 62. The average number of speeches in each debate was reported to be seven and this suggests that those who spoke at the debates in this era took a lot more time than today and were either already knowledgeable or well-prepared on the subject matter. The semi-public debate referred to was a continuing innovation. Invitations were doubtless issued to a number of local clubs and societies, but not to the general public.

The debate in 1866 which, according to the committee's report, 'soared above all the rest in the loftiness of the subject' was about Alpine climbing. The report stated that 'the motion that the present mania for Alpine climbing ought to be discountenanced by all sensible men was rejected by a large majority because of the eloquence of three members of the Alpine Club which was received with an avalanche of applause'. The three members of the Alpine Club were, in fact, the three members of the Mathews family in the society (Charles, George and William). This debate was much influenced by the challenge of the Matterhorn in Switzerland. An Englishman, Edward Whymper, had led the first successful assault in July 1865, but four of the party of seven lost their lives in the descent. This led to the Press fulminating pompously on the fruitless waste of life.

After the bombardment of puns on climbing, the joint honorary secretary, Alfred Browett, finished the committee's report with a flourish, stating that 'the shoals and quicksands which beset your society have been safely navigated and that a career of honour and usefulness is before it which time will but increase and make more lasting'. This over-effusive language by today's standards would have raised no eyebrows in that era. With the passage of time, speeches in debates, in the society or in parliament, would become more economical with words and form of expression. The time for anything else was simply running out. It is also interesting that, at one 1866 meeting, 21 new membership applications had to be dealt with. Most of them had Edgbaston addresses, but a lot of professional men at that time tended to give their business addresses for correspondence.

The subjects for debate remained elevated for years to come. It is clear that this generation of members had a greater knowledge of history than might be expected of those today, with perhaps some notable exceptions. The abstract or 'make of it what you will' motion which leads to no meaningful decision would not have been countenanced in the early years of the society. In 1867 there was a motion that 'the public policy and principles avowed by John Bright are favourable to the causes of true Liberalism'. Here again there is evidence of some support within the society for the radical tendency in the Liberal party. As it happened, the motion was defeated narrowly by 19 votes to 14. The majority of the society members remained politically Gladstonian and had not yet made common cause with the Tories.

CHAPTER 7

Lord Derby became prime minister in 1866. The second Reform Bill was passed in June 1867. The next year Benjamin Disraeli succeeded Derby as prime minister for the first time in a short-lived Conservative ministry. The Liberals won the 1868 election and William Gladstone became prime minister. The Franco-Prussian War broke out in 1870. France was defeated and was forced to cede Alsace, except Belfort, and most of Lorraine. The Conservatives, led by Disraeli, won an overall majority in the election of 1874. Transvaal was annexed in 1877 and the Zulu War started in 1879. The British were defeated at Isandlhwana.

By the opening of the 1867-68 session the membership had grown to 226. The numbers attending debates was the statistic that mattered, as the committee recognised, but this too was at levels unmatched before or since. Within two years the membership had risen to 240 and the two semi-public debates in the 1869-70 session attracted attendances of 160 and 205. But things remained patchy: one debate was adjourned because of a small attendance, a not unprecedented procedure. A new member in that session was Jesse Collings who became mayor in 1878, and later an MP and a Freeman of the City.

The subjects for debate were predominantly political at this time and this reflects a membership that was well-informed and took the trouble to be so. The rivalry between Gladstone and Disraeli was at its zenith and was followed avidly by the educated public through reports in the national newspapers. This undoubtedly was a factor in the resurgence of interest in the activities of the society. The committee report was able to refer approvingly to the standards of skill and eloquence in the society's debates.

The society debated, in November 1867, Garibaldi's action against the Papal States which was seen as an attack on the Pope's temporal power. Garibaldi was idolised by all classes of British society that sympathised with Italy's aspirations for nationhood and did not approve of the occupation by France and Austria. To European monarchies and governments, however, legitimacy mattered more in those days than self-determination. The society appeared to agree and did not approve of Garibaldi's revolutionary tendencies by 22 votes to 18.

In April 1868, the society debated female suffrage for the first time. The actual wording of the motion was 'female suffrage: a fallacy' and it was defeated by 24 votes to 21. As always, only the result was recorded when what was said in the debate would have been fascinating. It was a semi-public debate and there were 94 people present that day at the Assembly Rooms of Nock's Royal Hotel in Temple Row and it seems clear from the votes recorded, in this and many other debates, that there were considerable numbers of abstentions. The committee report submitted shortly afterwards expressed concern that the result of this debate on female suffrage was influenced unduly by the fact that ladies were present. The committee went so far as to suggest that the rules should be altered to introduce a secret ballot in order to prevent 'intimidation'! The same committee report also addressed the choice of motions for debate and expressed concern that they were, if anything, too focused on the political at the expense of the imaginative and philosophical.

Another trend since the society started has been the reduction in the time allowed for opening speeches from 40 to 30 minutes and from 20 minutes to 15 from the floor. It was proposed by Robert Francis Martineau that the president should have a bell which could be sounded one minute before a speaker's time was up. Guests had been welcomed to society meetings already and, whilst able to speak, could not vote. The laws were altered to allow ladies to be invited as guests. Nonetheless, the annual report of the committee made it clear that this arrangement was an experiment. The writer of the report, the honorary secretary Howard Smith, extolled both the advantages and disadvantages of ladies attending meetings. He wrote in a single sentence: 'We must not forget that, though the soft light of bright eyes may kindle in the breast of ardent and impetuous youth the ambition to distinguish himself, and that his efforts will be made stronger and his courage more indomitable by the consciousness that beauty is smiling upon him from an arm chair, yet there are more timid and retiring natures, who live to blush unseen, to whom these very circumstances act as a deterrent in trying their unpractised wings and only make more painful those fluttering and partial failures which must inevitably precede the acquisition of the power, to be obtained in so great a degree by practice, which will enable the possessor to take bold flights into the region of impassioned oratory and cleave his way into the highest realms of eloquence.'

In the 1869-70 session a semi-public debate attracted an attendance of 180. The motion compared George Eliot to Charles Dickens. Although George Eliot was amongst the finest of Victorian writers, one would have thought that she was up against it when compared to Dickens, and so it proved. That she in particular was named in the motion was a sop to the many ladies present seems highly probable and this risked a division on the basis of gender alone. But according to the records, the debate was of a high standard.

In March 1870 a motion was that variation of species is due to development rather than special acts of creation. This was the first time that the society had debated anything remotely relating to what is referred to in the records as the 'Darwinian hypothesis'. *The Origin of Species* had been published twelve years earlier and it led to a tempest of argument that has still not entirely quieted today, 150 years later. The fact that this motion was only carried by a single vote is, in itself, an indication that a group of supposedly down-to-earth Birmingham professional men could be on what most people today would consider to be the wrong side. Another motion shortly afterwards which targeted the restrictions imposed by the British Sunday was roundly defeated. This again indicates that the force of religious belief was still very strong.

By November the society had 255 members. A month later the short Franco-Prussian War had ended with France's surrender. The society debated whether the demand by Germany for the cession of Alsace and Lorraine as a condition of peace was both justifiable and politic. The society agreed that it was by 37 votes to 21. Whether this verdict coincided with the judgment of history is open to question.

A change in the laws was made that effectively allowed ladies to attend all debates of 'general interest'. The secretary would, in future, make it clear in his announcements whether ladies were to be admitted. What subjects were considered to be too sensitive for ladies is not clear from the minutes. One occasion considered suitable was an open debate at Nock's Royal Hotel on whether the existing legal, social and political position of English women was unjust and immoral. The house, including non-members in this case of course, agreed that it was by 64 votes to 42.

At the beginning of the session the location of meetings was moved from the Midland Institute to the Philosophical Theatre in Cannon Street. This led to complaints that there was too much air as opposed to too little and the acoustics were considered to be 'unexceptional'. The tiered seating of the theatre created an ambiance, which the secretary thought might try the nerves of 'younger and more bashful' speakers. However, the matter was resolved soon afterwards when the theatre was pulled down and the society returned to the Midland Institute.

One speaker in society debates who never could have been described as bashful was Joseph Chamberlain but, by this time, he had ceased to play any part in the life of the society. He was a progressive mayor of Birmingham from 1873 to 1876 (the mayor was chairman of the Council and its leader) and introduced many improvements including the municipalisation of gas and water, and slum clearance. He relinquished the office when he was elected to Parliament. He was the acknowledged leader of a breed of merchants and industrialists who both lived and worked in the city. They were citizens of the town who lived there or in one of its suburbs, and were not absentee capitalists who regarded Birmingham only as a workshop. In his time as mayor he received the Prince and Princess of Wales when they visited the town in June 1874. There was curiosity about how this would go as Chamberlain's radical reputation stretched to republicanism, but it all passed off smoothly. When he entered Parliament, he was already nationally well known.

A careful dresser with his monocle and orchid in his buttonhole, Chamberlain was cold and implacable, but was recognised from the outset as a politician of the front rank. The Liberals almost regarded with him with suspicion, perhaps justified eventually when he left the party to join the Conservatives years later. He was independent, formidable and politics became his life. He was Birmingham's first citizen and, when he changed parties because of his antipathy towards Home Rule, the entire city switched its political loyalties with him. He married three times. Austen, his eldest son by his first marriage, achieved high rank in the government between 1916 and 1929 and, in 1921, became leader of the Conservative MPs in the governing coalition led by Lloyd George. Austen was appointed Foreign Secretary in 1924. One of his sons by his second marriage, Neville, was to become Prime Minister in 1937. Both of Joseph's first two wives were members of the Kenrick family. The landed aristocracy would not have regarded Chamberlain as a gentleman, he was not in the Eton and Oxbridge mould, altogether too flash, too ambitious and with the taint of trade about him. Birmingham's standards in such matters were less demanding.

In 1872 the society debated whether the House of Lords as a hereditary body should be abolished. The motion was carried narrowly by nine votes to eight. At this time the upper house had a small but increasing Tory bias, and it was understandable that the society, with its Liberal leanings, delivered this verdict. Shortly afterwards home rule for Ireland was debated and rejected. This issue was to dominate politics in the last two decades of the nineteenth century and it might be observed that the society had got to grips with this issue before Parliament did.

The president in 1870-71, Dr John Langford, was asked to serve a second year - a 'first' for the amalgamated society. He was a distinguished man and, like John Thackray Bunce, a journalist and historian who, with careful antiquarianism, wrote *The Confiscation of Birmingham Guilds, Modern Birmingham, Handbook to the Educational Institutions of Birmingham* and *A Century of Birmingham Life* amongst other works. Bunce, however, was exceptional and some of his work was authored jointly with Samuel Timmins (for example *Memoir of Joseph Gillott*). All these men did not just write about the city as observers, they were involved. Langford and Timmins were on a committee formed to bring a public library to Birmingham. This had been made possible by the Free Libraries Act of 1850, but Birmingham lagged behind other boroughs in the country and it proved to be a frustrating task to achieve their objective against opposition from narrow economists.

Another change in the society rules at this time was a further shortening of the time allowed for opening speeches: it was now fixed at 15 minutes. A few years later speeches from the floor were limited to ten minutes maximum. The high level of attendance at debates had tapered off, but it was to return at the end of the decade. However, at this time concerns were again being expressed about the attendance at some of the debates. A debate in 1873 about the desirability of the gradual abolition of monarchical institutions produced a defeat for the motion by nine votes to two, a very modest attendance. This led to a committee proposal in February 1874 that any member who had not attended a debate for three years should be expelled. Past and present officers were to be exempted. A long and animated discussion followed which was inconclusive and unsupportive of the proposal. This led to an EGM only a week later at which the committee tendered its resignation *en bloc*.

The EGM expressed its confidence in the officers and committee and their resignation was withdrawn. The meeting then formed itself into a committee to discuss the situation. It was agreed that candidates for the committee should be nominated separately and not in a batch. This would allow a ballot. There was some other suggestions made and it was agreed that each candidate should be separately proposed, seconded and voted on. Whether this would have any effect on attendances was ignored. Nonetheless, the society reaffirmed its fundamental object: the cultivation and development of the art of public speaking. In spite of the increasing number of members, attendances were at a level which the committee found disheartening. Another cause for concern was that too few members were speaking in debates. The later report of the committee to members referred

These photographs of nineteenth century members were taken, of course, after they had ceased to be active in the society.

Alfred C. Osler   William Kenrick   Francis William Lowe   George Dixon

J. Thackray Bunce   John Alfred Langford   John Benjamin Stone   Jesse Collings

Robert Francis Martineau   Joseph Chamberlain   Sampson Gamgee   Thomas Martineau

Birmingham Debating Society.

LAWS

OF THE

BIRMINGHAM DEBATING SOCIETY,

PASSED AT

A MEETING HELD AT THE PHILOSOPHICAL INSTITUTION,

ON TUESDAY, THE THIRD DAY OF DECEMBER, 1850.

1.—That the Society shall be called "THE BIRMINGHAM DEBATING SOCIETY."

2.—That the office bearers shall consist of a Committee, Treasurer, and Secretary, who shall be elected at the Annual Meeting, which shall be held on the first Friday in October in each year.

3. That the Committee shall consist of seven persons, including the Secretary, three of whom shall be a quorum. They shall undertake the management of the general interests of the Society, and all questions for discussion shall be submitted to them before they are permitted to be debated.

4.—That the Committee may call Special General Meetings of the Society for the dispatch of special business.

5.—That all persons desirous of being admitted to the Society be first proposed and seconded by two members at an ordinary meeting, and their admission balloted for at

The laws of the second Birmingham Debating Society as agreed in 1850.

the next meeting: but they shall only be elected upon two-thirds of the members voting being in favour of their admission.

6.—That an annual subscription of ten shillings shall be paid by each member to the funds of the Society in advance.

7.—That the meetings shall be held fortnightly on Friday evenings, except during the months of June, July, August and September.

8.—That the hour of meeting shall be half-past seven o'clock: the Chairman to close the proceedings at ten o'clock, unless a majority of the members present wish to continue the business.

9.—That the Committee shall arrange with two members to open (pro and con) the discussion : but that whenever it is found desirable, the subject for discussion may be introduced by one member only.

10.—That a member first proposing a subject for discussion shall have the option of introducing it, if it be approved by the Committee. But that if the subject for discussion proposed by any member to the Committee be rejected by them, he may at any subsequent meeting take the opinion of the Society whether such subjects should be discussed.

11.—That the opening addresses may be read, but shall not exceed twenty minutes each, except by permission of the Chairman ; and every subsequent speaker shall be limited to fifteen minutes.

12.—That any member undertaking to open a subject

(pro or con) and failing to do so shall be fined five shillings: provided nevertheless that if necessarily absent from town on the night of meeting, or unable to attend, his subject may be introduced by another member.

13.—That the members may introduce gentlemen to the meetings of the Society, but no such visitors shall be entitled to join in the debates.

14.—That the Committee may make any meeting public when it shall seem advisable to them, and may previously appoint any person, whether a member or not, to take the chair on such occasion.

15.—That any member refusing to obey the decision of the Chairman, or violating the laws of the Society, may be expelled by the Committee : such member to have a right of appeal to the Society at an ordinary meeting, the decision of a majority of the members then present to be final.

16.—That no alteration shall be made in the laws except at an annual or special general meeting of the members ; notice of any proposed alteration having been given to the Society at an ordinary meeting one month previous to such meeting : reserving however to the Committee the power of suspending any of the laws they may see fit until an annual or special general meeting can be summoned, of which fourteen days' notice shall be given.

The laws of the second Birmingham Debating Society continued from facing page.

The ballot box.

Neville Chamberlain

David Brooks

LAWS

Birmingham and Edgbaston Debating Society.

NATURE OF THE SOCIETY.

1. This Society shall be called the "Birmingham and Edgbaston Debating Society," and its objects shall be the Discussion of any subjects, literary, political, historical, or other, except such as are of a theological character.

OF THE MEMBERS.

2. Candidates for admission into the Society shall be nominated, and their nomination seconded by Members; and a fortnight's notice shall be given to the Secretary of such nomination. In the case of the Annual General Meeting, such notice shall be given in writing; and in all other cases shall be given orally, at the Meeting preceding that at which such nomination shall be made.

3. New Members shall be admitted by Ballot. And no candidate for admission into the Society shall be considered elected, if one-fifth of the votes given by the Members present be unfavourable to such election.

4. Each Member shall pay in advance an Annual Subscription of 5s. Any Member neglecting to pay his Subscription within a fortnight after a second application by Circular, made by the Treasurer, shall cease to belong to the Society, and shall be informed of the same by the Secretary. Such person can then only be re-elected in the usual way, and after paying all Subscriptions due from him to the date of the proposed re-election.

5. Every Member shall be at liberty to introduce Gentlemen to the ordinary Meetings of the Society—and Gentlemen so introduced shall be allowed to speak on the subject of discussion, but take no other part in the proceedings of the Evening.

OF THE OFFICERS AND THE TRANSACTION OF BUSINESS.

6. The Officers of the Society shall be a President, a Vice-President, a Treasurer, a Secretary, and a Committee, and all such Officers shall be elected at the Annual General Meeting, which shall be the first Meeting of the Session, and shall be held on the first Wednesday in October in each year.

7. The Committee shall have full power to fix the times for the meetings of the Society—to arrange the subjects for its discussion—and generally to regulate its proceedings; but not to admit new Members, nor make any alteration in or addition to the permanent laws of the Society.

8. The Committee shall consist of Five Members, in addition to the President, Vice-President, Treasurer, and Secretary, who shall be ex-officio Members of it.

9. The Secretary shall preserve minutes of each Meeting of the Society, and of the Committee: and in the minutes of every Meeting of the Society shall be entered—the names of the Chairman and the other Members present—the business transacted—the subject debated—the names of the Speakers of each side—and the result of the division at the conclusion of the debate.

10. For the transaction of business at any Meeting of the Society the presence of six Members shall be necessary, and the Debate shall not commence until the business is concluded.

The laws of the Birmingham & Edgbaston Debating Society in 1858.

IV

11. No motion involving any alteration in or addition to the laws of the Society, or otherwise affecting its permanent constitution, shall be made at any Meeting, without a fortnight's notice being given to the Secretary, specifying the terms of such motion. In the case of the Annual General Meeting, such notice shall be given in writing, and in all other cases shall be given orally, at the Meeting preceding that at which such motion shall be made.

12. All notices of motion and nomination of Members shall be inserted in the circulars.

OF THE CHAIRMAN.

13. The Chair shall be occupied at each Meeting by the President, or the Vice-President; and in case both these Officers should be absent, the Chairman for the Evening shall be elected by the Members present.

14. The Chairman shall have unlimited authority in every question of order—shall be sole interpreter of the laws—and in all cases of an equality of votes shall have a casting vote.

OF THE MEETINGS.

15. The ordinary Meetings of the Society shall be held every alternate Wednesday during the Session, the hour of Meeting shall be Half-past Seven o'clock, and the Debate shall not continue after Half-past Ten. But the times of Meeting shall be subject to any such temporary alteration as the Committee shall make from time to time.

16. No Member shall be allowed to speak twice on the subject of discussion (unless by way of explanation) until every Member desirous of speaking has done so: but the opener shall be permitted to make a reply at the conclusion of the Debate.

17. No Member shall be allowed to speak more than twenty minutes, except the openers on either side, who shall be allowed forty minutes each.

18. Any Member neglecting to speak first or second upon a subject which he has undertaken, and failing to find a substitute, shall pay a fine of Five Shillings, which it shall be in the power of the Society to remit.

19. That Public Meetings of the Society may be held at such times, and subject to such regulations as the Committee may appoint.

Sealed 17. Nov. 1858

C. Mathews

Hon. Sec.

Birmingham and Edgbaston Debating Society.

71 TEMPLE ROW,
BIRMINGHAM,
May, 1902.

DEAR SIR,

The **Summer Meeting** will be held on Saturday, June 21st, at

WELLINGTON, WROXETER, AND THE WREKIN.

The following Programme has been arranged :—Cold Luncheon will be provided in a room which has been reserved on the up platform at Snow Hill Station from 12 o'clock until the departure of the train for Wellington. Members will leave Snow Hill Station from the down platform (Saloons or Reserved Carriages) by the 12-48 train due Wellington at 1-43.

On arrival at Wellington the party will drive to Wroxeter to view the ruins of Uriconium. Arrangements have been made to go over the ruins, and for Guide Books to be supplied. The party will then drive through Uppington, and thence to the foot of the Wrekin.

Tea will be provided here at the Forest Glen Pavilion. After tea the party will make the ascent of the Wrekin, at the top of which other refreshments will be provided. A magnificent view can be obtained from the summit. On descending the hill conveyances will await the party and drive to the Wrekin Hotel, Wellington, where dinner will be served at 7-15 p.m.

The train leaves for Birmingham at 8-42 p.m.

Members will please observe the following time table, to which we have strictly to adhere :—

Train leaves Birmingham (Snow Hill)	12-48 p.m.
Train arrives Wellington	1-43 ,,
Leave for Wroxeter	1-50 ,,
Arrive at Wroxeter (Uriconium)	2-50 ,,
Leave Wroxeter	3-30 ,,
Arrive The Wrekin (Forest Glen Pavilion)	4-30 ,,
Start for Summit	5-0 ,,
Return Forest Glen Pavilion	6-40 ,,
Drive to Wellington	6-45 ,,
Dinner at The Wrekin Hotel, Wellington	7-15 ,,
Train leaves Wellington	8-42 ,,
Train arrives Birmingham (Snow Hill)	10-26 ,,

Short particulars of the places of interest will be found on the fly-leaf.

Tickets, 8/- each for Members, and 14/- each for Visitors, may be now obtained from me, and a form of application is enclosed.

An early application is requested, in order that the necessary arrangements may be made with the Railway Company and others.

Yours faithfully,

BERTRAM O. PEMBERTON,
Hon. Secretary.

Society outings were meticulously organised with printed tickets and planned travel.

Birmingham and Edgbaston Debating Society.

... Summer Meeting. ...

Wellington, Wroxeter, and The Wrekin,

On Saturday, 21st June, 1902.

Leave Snow Hill Station	12·48 p.m.
Arrive Wellington	1·43 p.m.
Depart Wellington	8·42 p.m.
Arrive Snow Hill, Birmingham	10·26 p.m.

Member's Ticket.

BERTRAM O. PEMBERTON, Hon. Sec.

Birmingham and Edgbaston Debating Society.

SUMMER MEETING.

WELLINGTON, WROXETER, and THE WREKIN.

Members who have not yet applied for Tickets are particularly requested to do so by MONDAY next, as otherwise sufficient accommodation cannot be ensured.

N.B.—Date, Saturday, 21st June. Tickets: Members, 8/-; Visitors, 14/-. Leave Snow Hill Station for Wellington, 12-48 p.m. Lunch provided at Station before you leave.

Yours faithfully,

BERTRAM O. PEMBERTON,

71 *Temple Row,*   *Hon. Sec.*
12th June, 1902.

Birmingham and Edgbaston Debating Society. ...

Summer Meeting, 1902.

Luncheon

To be given up to the Attendant at the Refreshment Room Snow Hill Station.

Ticket . .

Laws of the
Edgbaston Debating Society

Nature of the Society

1. This Society shall be called the "Edgbaston Debating Society", and its object shall be the discussion of any subjects literary, political, historical, or other, except such as are of a theological character –

Of the Members.

2. Candidates for admission into the Society shall be nominated, and their nomination seconded by Members – and no such nomination shall be made at any meeting except the annual general meeting, unless oral notice thereof shall have been given at the meeting immediately preceding that on which such nomination shall be made

3. New Members shall be admitted by Ballot – And no Candidate for admission into the Society shall be considered elected, if one fifth of the votes given by the members present be unfavourable to such election –

4. Each Member shall pay in advance an annual subscription of five shillings, except when elected a Member of the Society after the first of February, when the subscription for the current year shall be three shillings

5. Every Member shall be at liberty to introduce Gentlemen to the ordinary meetings of the Society, and Gentlemen so introduced shall be allowed to speak on the subject of discussion, but to take no other part in the proceedings of the Evening –

Of the Officers and the transaction of business

6. The Officers of the Society shall be a President, a Vice President a Treasurer, a Secretary, and a Committee, and all such Officers shall be elected at the annual general meeting which shall be the first meeting of the Session, and shall be held on the first Wednesday in October in each Year

7. The Committee shall have full power to fix the times for the

The first page of the laws of the Edgbaston Debating Society
(as revised by the committee in 1853).

to 'infusing new life' into the society, but its tone was sombre and discouraged. However, at the AGM in October 1875 at the Midland Hotel in New Street, the committee's reports were more upbeat than the previous year's. More members, it stated, were supporting debates and speaking.

The Conservative party led by Benjamin Disraeli won the 1874 General Election and had an overall majority for the first time since 1846. The society debated whether a Conservative government at the present time would be a national disadvantage. The vote was 12 - 12 and the chairman gave his casting vote to the affirmative. This is the type of motion on which every member will vote according to his political loyalties and it suggests that the society was equally divided between Conservative and Liberal sympathisers.

A motion that Professor Tyndall's recent hypothesis of matter was not antagonistic to true religion was carried by 51 votes to eight. The hypothesis was that everything in the world could be traced back to molecules of matter that interacted with each other. The arguments deployed against were similar to those that would have been used against Charles Darwin. John Tyndall, an Irishman, was a great teacher of natural philosophy and an explorer of nature. He ranks with Darwin and Huxley.

The society agreed to move from the poorly ventilated Midland Institute and settled on the Albert Chambers. The committee felt that this move had helped the 'clouds to lift' but its report on the 1876-77 session expressed concern about a backwardness of some members in putting themselves forward to speak. The report pointed out that leading lights in the society in the past had also played a leading part in the corporate and cultural life of Birmingham. Present members were exhorted to do more. There were 288 members at this time. A new innovation, the impromptu debate was introduced with speakers drawn by ballot provided that they had agreed to participate. Unlike today's impromptu debates, every speaker from the floor, and the side he was required to take, was decided by a ballot. This meant that members faced the challenge of speaking against their own convictions.

The report also stated that the average attendance was 56, a good number, but there were, also on average, only eight speakers in each debate. It referred to the low point which was an attendance of 22 with only five speeches. The motions for debate were, as usual, political, educational and theological. An interesting subject for one debate was that *Daniel Deronda* was unworthy of the reputation of George Eliot. As this novel, written in 1876, could be regarded as one of her finest works, it is surprising that such a critical motion could be put to the house so soon after it was first published.

During the same session a lady was proposed as a member. This was unprecedented and the committee had little idea about how to deal with the matter. It was agreed that the matter should be discussed by the whole society. However, the nomination was withdrawn before matters went any further. This can now be seen as the first shot in a campaign that did not end until the twenty-first century.

A problem arose in 1877 because the president's address had been printed, as was often the case, and words had been included to the effect that the publication had been printed in the name of the society at the request of the committee and with the permission of several named members. It was pointed out that something could not be 'printed by the society' without the approval of the society itself - the full membership, not the committee. The matter was discussed at a meeting and the point was carried by a majority of 27 votes to 19. The point was a minor but principled one and the committee felt it had been acting in accordance with the wishes of the membership. The matter got quite animated when certain members of the committee voted in disapproval of their own actions.

One hundred and fifty people attended a semi-public debate in 1878 and the motion was 'that the theory of human will as propounded by Professor Tyndall (in a recent address at the Midland Institute) is erroneous and inimical to morality'. It was carried by 60 votes to 24. Clearly the vote of the society three years earlier (see above) did not influence this larger and apparently less enlightened gathering.

An interesting motion for another semi-public meeting in 1878 was 'that the present system of political organisation best ascertains and secures the carrying out of the voice or the wishes of the majority; it is the most effectual means by which any great good as regards legislation can be effected and it is unobjectionable on moral grounds'. The negative, therefore, had to make the case for universal suffrage without qualification (except for age and sex). Britain in 1878 was not a democratic country in the sense we understand it today. No more than 20 percent of adult male population had a vote and the Third Reform Bill was still six years away. Members of the society would have had the vote by now, but the belief that government was the business of an informed elite, of which they were now part, was deeply ingrained in their thinking. The motion was carried narrowly by 25 votes to 24.

The committee's report of the 1877-78 session was encouraging. It stated that more members were speaking in debates, but that the motions had been rendered much less difficult. Membership had held steady at 288, but the average attendance rose to 65. This was about as good as it gets, better than anything before or since. The suffrage was again debated in this session and again the result was close. The committee report questioned whether too many political issues were pervading the subjects chosen for debate. However, it was generally felt that the close results of the debates justified it. Generally, the verdicts delivered in political debates reflected an increasingly Conservative bias on most issues: anti-trade union and pro-corporal punishment for example

Concern was expressed about a report of a meeting appearing in the Press without the sanction of the committee. The assumption that the committee had a sanction to prevent anything appearing in the Press seems a little naïve. The society began meeting at King Edward's Grammar School in New Street in 1879, with semi-public meetings being held at the Grand Hotel in Colmore Row.

In April 1881 the society looked at the conduct of debates. It was proposed and seconded that the first speaker in the negative should confine himself to answering the argument of the opening speech, and that subsequent speakers, without precluding their right to raise new points, should still try to keep their observations relevant to preceding speakers. The motion was discussed at length, but was eventually withdrawn without a vote being taken. However, the point was well made and the problem has been mentioned already in this narrative. If speakers are merely going to say what they came to say regardless of what has gone before or any thread of argument, the quality of debate will suffer. On the other hand, it can be argued that proposers should not be allowed to define a motion within narrow limits of their own choosing and thus stifle wider-ranging contributions.

The society also faced up to the fact that it had a lot of members who were members in name only. The disparity between the average attendance and the total membership was marked. Resolutions were introduced again demanding the expulsion of members who had not attended debates in three years. Another resolution targeted those who had not spoken for three years. After lengthy discussion, all resolutions and amendments were dropped, but it was felt that the discussion had reminded members of their responsibilities to the society. Membership exceeded 300 around this time, but the average attendance was falling. The committee became worried about the poor support from younger members. Amongst the changes suggested was that members of the committee should lead by example and undertake to attend every debate. This demanding requirement was eventually carried as an amendment to the laws in November 1882. One can only presume from thereon that the spirit, rather than the letter, of this law was what counted.

A ladies' debating society was formed in Edgbaston in 1881. Wives and daughters of the members of the Birmingham & Edgbaston Debating Society predominated and the first president was the wife of Alfred Osler (who was to be president of BEDS in 1884-85). Three as yet unmarried girls from the Chamberlain family were members. Others prominent in the early stages were Mrs Arthur Phillp (wife of the BEDS president 1878-79) and Mrs Ralph Heaton. Needless to say, a lady in those days would only be referred to by her husband's first name and not her own!

In 1890 the society became the Ladies' Literary & Debating Society which suggests a change of emphasis. In the organisation of debates, the society followed the pattern of its 'elder brother'. Retiring presidents delivered valedictory addresses and some of these were exceptional, particularly one on the merits of Robert Browning's poetry. The ladies' society fizzled out in 1911. It is not unusual for some momentum to be lost after the early burst of enthusiasm. In 1911, the suffragette agitation was at its peak but it is difficult to conclude whether this might have been a factor.

It would, of course, have been unthinkable in the 1880s for ladies to join the all male Birmingham & Edgbaston Debating Society as members. This had little or nothing to do with their intellectual capacities, but simply because men preferred their own company, and to smoke. Ladies had attended public and other selected debates from soon after the society had been founded.

CHAPTER 8

In 1882 there was a military rising in Egypt under Arabi Pasha. The British won a victory at Tel-el-Kebir. General Gordon died in Khartoum in 1885 as the British evacuated Sudan. Gladstone's ministry fell and Lord Salisbury became prime minister for the first time. The Liberals were returned with a majority in 1886, but a Home Rule bill was defeated and the Conservatives won another election. They remained in power until 1892.

Weighty subjects were debated in the 1882-83 session such as the English Reformation, whether Arabi Pasha's rising was a national movement, aestheticism and the merits of the novel *John Inglesant*. The latter had been written and published in 1881 by a Birmingham manufacturer, Henry Shorthouse, and it contributed a unique synthesis of Anglo-Catholic sensibilities to the legacy of the Oxford Movement. Arabi Pasha was an Egyptian nationalist leader who eventually was defeated at the Battle of Tel-el-Kebir in 1882. One cannot but be impressed that members were well enough informed to debate motions such as these. Another interesting motion in the same session was that 'no consistent Liberal can now support the Liberal Party'. The Liberals had come to power in 1880 following a negative electoral campaign offering little more than an end to 'Beaconsfieldism' (Disraeli was by then the Earl of Beaconsfield) and the party lacked coherent direction as a result. Things were also particularly bad in Ireland. However, the motion was lost by eleven votes to five as was probably inevitable with this uncompromising wording.

There were a number of distinguished men who became presidents of the society during this epoch. Most of them were in the professions and amongst their number was Howard S. Smith (1872-73), a chartered accountant. The firm he founded was to be taken over by Price Waterhouse nearly 100 years later. Others were H. Lakin Smith (1876-77) who was also a chartered accountant and a partner in his firm; Francis Lowe (1879-80), a solicitor and property developer who became a Member of Parliament and was knighted; the Reverend E. F. M. McCarthy was a distinguished headmaster; Joseph Sampson Gamgee (1883-84) was a famous surgeon and founder of the Birmingham Hospital Saturday Fund, and Jordan Lloyd (1891-92) was a very distinguished oculist.

There was concern expressed at the AGM that year that some members of the society spoke and then left before the vote. The fact that many participating in debates were only using them as an opportunity to practice their rhetoric before a live audience is not something that they should have made too obvious. If a debate is a contest between two polarised opinions, one is letting one's own side down by leaving early. After all, votes are the only measure by which victory or defeat is decided. The point has been made in the introduction to this book that passion and a polarisation of views adds to a debate. The matter was discussed at the AGM where concern was expressed that the motions for debate were 'only mild propositions' and that, as a result, the 'temperature' of the discussions was too low. The members demanded that 'more life into the proceedings' be injected.

Attention was also drawn in the annual report to the fact that the society had instructed many members into becoming good speakers and this was demonstrated by the distinction they had achieved in their careers. The report raised the possibility that the day of debating societies might have gone by and then refuted its own suggestion by referring to the fact that there were so many subjects to discuss. The report concluded that, if there was a problem, it centred on the perennial issue of attendance levels.

The subjects debated in the 1883-84 session were again weighty - on matters such as education policy, a British protectorate over Egypt, whether there had been any great development in English literature since the death of Milton and if writers and poets should be rewarded with peerages. In one debate the society decided that town life was more conducive to happiness than living in the country. As all or nearly all of the members were town rather than country dwellers, this comes as no surprise. The annual report again expressed concern about attendance. This did not apply to the two semi-public debates, one of which attracted over 300 people. The fact is that all societies, whatever their purposes, tend to be disappointed with the support they get from members and will frequently complain of 'apathy'. However, there will always be long-term fluctuations and these serve as a reminder to committees to take positive steps to prevent what might otherwise become a serious decline in support.

At the start of 1884-85 session, the annual report of the committee stated that there were 251 members and the average attendance of members at ordinary meetings was 33. This was considered to be too low and the committee's solution was a proposal to allow smoking as it was felt that this might increase attendance among younger men. From thereon, there were one or two smoking debates in every session. In those days, however, to smoke in the presence of ladies would have been unthinkable, but there were no lady members. Nonetheless, ladies could attend the semi-public debates and an increasing number of the ordinary meetings as visitors, so smoking would not have been acceptable at those meetings. To accept ladies as full members of the society was a too progressive idea at this time: the generally held opinion was that they might inhibit the more vigorous elements of debate. In its report, the committee expressed the hope that, when allowed to attend, they would 'not alter the character of the society's meetings'. Until this point in time, there was no record in the minutes of a woman having spoken in a semi-public debate.

In November 1884 it was agreed to admit the Press to debates. This meant primarily *The Birmingham Daily Post* and, as mentioned earlier, its long-serving editor, John Thackray Bunce, happened to be a member of the society and a former president. The reports of debates subsequently were thorough and detailed in a way that would be inconceivable today. There were no mass-circulation tabloids in those days and the newspapers then were written for the educated classes. Popular journalism was still 20 years in the future.

From 1884-85 onwards a joint meeting with Birmingham Central Literary Association became a regular feature of every annual session. Like the other debates, these were held at the Grand Hotel, Colmore Row, in Birmingham's city centre. The BCLA had been formed in 1855 and the vote counts recorded in the joint debates with the society suggest that the former body was the more radical.

The committee's report at the next AGM advised that there were 248 members and that the average attendance at debates was 77. The latter figure was double that of the previous year's and one is bound to wonder if the semi-public and joint debates were included in the calculation this time.

A debate that the unemployed must always be cared for was lost, and this indicates that the society's political character was becoming increasingly Conservative. Whilst many in the party would argue for one-nation Toryism at that time, the right-left divide was becoming increasingly apparent and hostility to trade union activity was stronger in Conservative ranks than in those of the Liberal party. Nonetheless a motion in support of the Conservative government was lost by only one vote (members only) but was carried by members and visitors.

At the end of the session the committee's report was a rallying call to members. They were firmly asked to support the society more and to speak when invited to do so. The point was again made by the committee that the society provided training for participation in the municipal life of the town. It is a sad fact in a way that the city's leading businessmen today are not to be found serving on the city's council. The frenetic pace of business life now makes that almost impossible, but this was not the case in the nineteenth century. Of course, men who ran businesses could give themselves time off for civic duty. The working-class councillor was still an impossible contradiction.

The Conservative party, which now included the Liberal Unionists, had gained power in 1885 and Lord Salisbury's first administration fell in 1886. A Home Rule bill was defeated and at the general election which followed, the Conservatives and Liberal Unionists gained a substantial majority. The increasing use of the name 'Unionist Party' indicated how important the issue of Ireland was in the last two decades of the nineteenth century and the first two of the twentieth. It also took into account the sensitivities of some Liberal MPs who were against Home Rule and had changed their party allegiance as a result.

Home rule was Gladstone's last great cause and it tore the Liberal party apart. There were Liberal Unionists who would vote against their own party whenever Home Rule was debated, and Liberal Imperialists led by Lord Rosebery who could recognise the inconsistency of seeking to build an empire and at the same time being prepared to give part of it away. A new generation of Liberals such as Asquith, Grey and Haldane realised the dangers of Home Rule being the only issue for the party. The biggest loss for the Liberals in 1886 was Joseph Chamberlain who saw his future to be with the Conservatives. For the imperialist Chamberlain, Home Rule meant little more than a limited extension of Irish self-government whereas, for Gladstone, it meant an Irish parliament. The society debated a motion in 1886 in favour of Home Rule and it was lost.

Until the late 1870s the Conservative party had no political organisation in Birmingham and its suburbs. One man who played a part in changing that was John Benjamin Stone. He had resigned from the debating society in 1874 and he devoted the next six years to building a party organisation in the city that had previously been based only on clubs such as the Birmingham Conservative Club. Stone later became Member of Parliament for East Birmingham and was knighted. He was the first mayor of Sutton Coldfield and a pioneer in photography and a collector of mosses, pursuits he could follow thanks to the success of his father as a manufacturer. He was the great-grandfather of Roger Stone, a former president and the current secretary of the society.

The 1887 AGM was followed by dinner at the Grand Hotel with 70 members attending. After dinner, the usual valedictory address was given by the outgoing president, Fowler Carter, on the somewhat esoteric subject of the second part of Goethe's *Faust*. In January 1888 the society debated jointly with the Birmingham Central Literary Association whether the government's Irish policies were doomed to failure. The motion was lost by 80 votes to 52. The government at the time was Conservative (or Unionist) led by Lord Salisbury and the fact remains that the proposer was right: the Conservative policies on Ireland were doomed to failure. The government's Irish policy was debated again a year later and it was supported by the society. There was nothing more noble in the politics of the time than Gladstone's efforts, when he was in power, to win Home Rule for Ireland. The refusal of the Conservative majority in the House of Lords to countenance it was discreditable and a high price was to be paid. The verdict of the debating society probably accorded with public opinion at the time.

A motion, which effectively amounted to a call for the Corn Laws to be re-introduced, was defeated by members but carried when visitors' votes were taken into account. The annual report of the committee commented later that the enthusiastic and reactionary visitors had outweighed the 'openness of mind and sweet reasonableness' of the members. Towards the end of the session, there was an impromptu debate on the enfranchisement of women. This was defeated. In a notice of an impromptu debate 20 years later, the procedure to be followed was to be laid down. One must presume that what was to be written many years later (in 1909) merely codified that which had been agreed for this and other impromptu debates. It was required that the openers speak for ten minutes, other speakers for not more than five minutes each. The names of the other speakers were to be drawn from a hat as the debate proceeds, but only of those who had consented to speak. Those whose names were drawn out of the hat were required to speak alternately for affirmative or negative even if they found themselves forced to argue against their own firmly held convictions.

Meetings in the 1888-89 session took place at the Great Western Hotel in Colmore Row, no more than a stone's throw from the Grand. This change of location might have been in the interests of economy and subsequently several venues were to be tried until the society moved its meetings back to the Grand in 1894 where they continued until the 1960s. At the beginning of the session it was suggested that reports to the local newspapers should not include the names of the speakers. This was overruled on a show of hands and the minute does not clarify the reason why there was concern on this point. Perhaps it was a matter of confidentiality relating to the political opinions of speakers. It was one thing, of course, for the society to write its own reports for the press in the hope that they would be published, but quite another if reporters attended meetings. In the latter instance, they would write what they liked as they were entitled to do.

Motions continued to follow the political and social issues of the time. In March 1889 a semi-public debate again considered Home Rule. It was defeated by 70 votes to 34. Whilst the Unionist majority in the House of Lords could be blamed for frustrating the will of the Commons on Home Rule, it could claim with justification that public opinion was on its side. With no public opinion polls in those days, the society's vote might have been as good a 'barometer' as any other.

The joint debates with the Birmingham Central Literary Association remained a consistent annual feature of the society's programme for several decades. The motion in this session was that steps should be taken to establish a Midlands university. It was only just carried by 39 votes to 35. Capital punishment was debated at the next meeting, but the motion did not require a straight yes or no. Instead, it alluded to the difficulties of the Florence Maybrick case - a shocking miscarriage of justice at the time - and stated that the ultimate punishment was not appropriate when evidence was circumstantial. Unsurprisingly, the supporters of capital punishment were not disposed to consider any compromise. In 1889 one motion debated by the society was that 'to be or not to be, that is the question'. It is not clear what the drafters of the motion intended. Was suicide in some way the issue?

Valedictory addresses given at AGMs by the outgoing president were continued until towards the end of the twentieth century. The subjects were esoteric and typical was that of Henry Lee in 1889, who spoke on the decay of dogmatic theology. The following year Dr Showell Rogers delivered his address on the legal aspects of English fiction. Jordon Lloyd spoke two years later on 'some errors of civilisation from the medical standpoint'. Notable a generation later (in the late 1920s and early 1930s) were Norman Wall's address on romance in literature, Thomas Kennedy's on language reform, Wilfred Matthews's on utopias old and new, and Wynne Frazier's 'serious reflections upon humour'. These are just a number of examples of the weighty subject matter. All these later valedictory addresses were printed and those who made them prepared their material with care. The last to be made was in 1996.

CHAPTER 9

Kaiser Wilhelm II succeeded to the throne of Germany in 1888 and Bismarck was dismissed two year later. The new emperor visited England five times between 1890 and 1894. Gladstone's last ministry was from 1892 to 1894. He was succeeded by the Earl of Rosebery in 1894, but the latter lost power in 1895. The third Salisbury administration lasted from 1895 to 1901. In 1896 the Jameson raid into the Transvaal failed and Cecil Rhodes resigned the premiership of Cape Colony.

The French Revolution was debated in 1889, its centenary year. It is an interesting thought that whilst no members of the society would have been alive at the time, the elderly amongst them would, in their youth, have known family and friends who were and been able to recall first-hand the events of 1789. In the same way, most of the senior members of the society today have known veterans of the 1914-18 war.

The regular joint debate with the Birmingham Central Literary Association considered the inequalities in society. The vote was 65 to 30 in favour of government action. An interesting motion in December 1890 was 'that private fortunes built up of rents and interest are part of a gigantic system for the misappropriation of national wealth'. This proposition could be said to put forward a rather naïve viewpoint of how the economy worked. It was defeated and the committee report at the end of the session was to state that a number of members stayed away that night because they considered that to debate a motion of such socialistic tendency was immoral in itself. The report added that, whilst the society was prepared to discuss motions of this type, the defeat of a proposition of 'such enormity' was reassuring.

The next motion debated in the session was that the modern system of mural advertisement is degrading to the public and injurious to public morals. This was also defeated. Both motions suggest that an anti-capitalist faction existed within the society. There were debates on trade unionism, the Salvation Army, brewery tied houses and shortening the working day. Intoxicating liquor was a big issue in those days and the teetotallers were able to muster a majority in the tied houses debate by suggesting that brewery ownership of tied houses was the main element in the 'evils of the drink traffic'.

At the end of the session the committee proposed some constitutional changes, most particularly that the time allocated to speakers should be shortened. This was carried after considerable discussion. The process of shortening the time allocation allowed to all speakers in debates was an almost continual one. It was not so much a consequence of the level of attendance, but from the desire of more of those present to speak in debates.

The semi-public debate in November 1891 attracted 250 people to the Temperance Hall in Temple Street. The motion was that 'the use of the bible as a day school textbook in board schools is religiously injurious' and it was carried by a narrow majority. At a following meeting the society discussed whether Latin and Greek should be compulsory in university and professional examinations. It decided that they should be and struck a blow for classical education.

In January 1892 the society recorded its sympathy with the Prince and Princess of Wales on the death of their eldest son, Albert Victor, the Duke of Clarence, who died of influenza. Whether any further action was taken is not recorded in the minutes. 'Prince Eddy' as he was known has become a largely forgotten historical figure and the target for a certain amount of inconclusive speculation. But in 1892 that sort of thing never got into the Press and members of the debating society would have known nothing of it. His demise paved the way for George V to become king in 1910.

The joint meeting with the Birmingham Central Literary Association discussed the motion that 'the socialistic ideal foreshadowed in Alfred Hayes's poem *The March of Man* is desirable and attainable'. The room was so full that some members could not get in. The society members carried the motion, but it was lost on the vote of members and visitors.

Meetings in the 1892-93 session were held at 7a Newhall Street in Birmingham's city centre. Home Rule was debated yet again by the society and defeated by a three-quarters majority. The committee report described the result as a foregone conclusion but the matter was frequently debated by the society because it was much the most important political issue of the time. Gladstone was still Prime Minister but even his own party were not all Little Englanders. The Liberal imperialists were led by the Earl of Rosebery, who was soon to become Prime Minister (1894-95). The first debate in 1893 was again about Home Rule. In this case, the motion was that the House of Lords was justified in rejecting the bill. This was carried by a wide margin.

With meetings back at the Grand Hotel in 1894, the society debated the power of the House of Lords to veto measures passed by the Commons. The society decided, by a very substantial majority, that the Lords should keep its powers. The Liberal Lord Rosebery was Prime Minister at this time and the fact that a Tory dominated House of Lords could and did frustrate government legislation was an issue that would have to be tackled sooner or later. Now was not the time and Ireland was not the right issue. In 1895 the Liberals lost power for ten years and the battle to come was thus postponed.

In March there was a joint debate with the Oxford Union Society. This was the first time that the Oxford Union had involved itself in a joint debate with any society apart from with its opposite number at Cambridge University. Only five undergraduates came, but they made four of the six opening speeches and played a prominent part. The motion was 'that the increasing power of democracy is to be viewed with apprehension' and it was carried by 73 votes to 49. This may seem surprising today but, even after three Reform Bills, only a minority of men and no women had the vote. At this time the nation's elite still believed that the task of running the country was its exclusive preserve and the possibility of the socialistic masses having the vote was a frightening spectre indeed!

CHAPTER 10

In 1899 the Transvaal attempted to become a sovereign state, but Joseph Chamberlain, the Colonial Secretary, refused to admit the claim and the Boer War started in October. There were British setbacks until Lord Roberts was appointed commander-in-chief and Lord Kitchener chief-of-staff. Roberts occupied Pretoria in May 1900 and then handed over command to Kitchener. Queen Victoria died in January 1901. Guerilla tactics were adopted by the Boers and Kitchener used concentration camps and blockhouses to overcome them. The Peace of Vereeniging was signed in May 1902. Lord Salisbury retired as prime minister and was succeeded by Arthur Balfour.

With the forthcoming celebrations of 50 years in the life of the society, Joseph Chamberlain was invited to be president for a second time after a gap of over 30 years. The celebrations actually commemorated the year that the Edgbaston Debating Society and the first Birmingham Debating Society were founded individually, not the formation of the amalgamated society in 1855. It was almost ten years since Chamberlain had left the Liberal party and joined the Conservatives who accepted him into their ranks with some suspicion, but his abilities could not be gainsaid. Chamberlain accepted the society's invitation to be president in this special year, but made it clear that he did not have time to take the chair at ordinary meetings. As a result, Thomas Ryland, the vice-president, took the chair more often than not. Thomas Ryland was one of five members of his family who became members of the society in the nineteenth century. As mentioned earlier in this narrative, the prominent Birmingham legal firm Ryland & Martineau had been formed when Thomas Martineau joined Arthur Ryland in 1852. Neither Thomas Ryland nor any other members of the family were to join the practice and it is now called Martineau Johnson (following a merger in 1987). Thomas Martineau had died in 1893 and therefore did not live to see the golden jubilee celebrations of the society that he had played such a prominent part in forming.

There were 274 members at the beginning of the session and it rose to 306 during it. The average attendance was around 50. As part of the celebrations, a register was compiled listing all members since the formation of the society, and of the two separate societies before the amalgamation.

This was presented to the society by the committee. Compiling it had been a painstaking task, undertaken in copper-plate handwriting by David Brooks, secretary from 1894 to 1896, and later president (1900-01). David Brooks was to serve as Lord Mayor of Birmingham from 1916 to 1918 when he was knighted. He became a Freeman of Birmingham in 1923. The register shows that there were sixteen members who had been Mayor of Birmingham: Henry Wiggin (1864), George Dixon (1866), Joseph Chamberlain (1873-75), William Kenrick (1877), Jesse Collings (1878), Richard Chamberlain (1879-80), Thomas Martineau (1886), George Johnson (1893) and Thomas Fallows (1894). After incorporation in 1895, Lord Mayors from the society included Charles Gabriel Beale (1897-99 and 1904), Hallewell Rogers (1902-03), Henry James Sayer (1906-07), George Hamilton Kenrick (1908), Ernest Martineau (1912-13), Neville Chamberlain (1915-16), David Brooks (1916-18) and George Corbyn Barrow (1965-66). As well as David Brooks, Thomas Martineau, Hallewell Rogers and George Kenrick were also knighted. Today, however, busy doctors, lawyers and hands-on businessmen no longer have the time for civic duty. The character and age profile of the members have changed over the years and whether the society will produce national or local politicians in the future is doubtful.

In 1896 the dinner to celebrate the golden jubilee of the society took place at the Grand Hotel in Birmingham presided over by Joseph Chamberlain. Twenty-five former presidents attended including Thomas Watts who had been president of the Edgbaston Debating Society in 1854-55 before the merger with Birmingham. There were also six members of the original Edgbaston Debating Society present: Surgeon-Major Henry Greenhow, Benjamin Mathews, Councillor Robert Francis Martineau, Edward Peyton, John Barlow and Edmund Blyth. Guests of the society included the Lord Mayor, the presidents of the Oxford and Cambridge Unions, the US Consul and the president of the Birmingham Central Literary Association. 148 'visitors' also dined with the members making a total of 333 in all. There were several toasts, including to the president, Joseph Chamberlain, who had earlier delivered an address on the art of public speaking.

Anyone familiar with the history of Birmingham will recognise names in the list of those present who were antecedents of men who played a part in the commercial life of the city for generations afterwards, names such as Ryland, Martineau, Ansell, Deeley, Rubery, Sharp, Whitlock, Osler, Wolseley and Fyshe. Chamberlain's address received widespread press coverage on the very next day. That it should be written up in the *Birmingham Daily Post* and in the other local papers (*Birmingham Daily Argus, Birmingham Daily Gazette* and *Birmingham Daily Mail*) would have been expected, but it was also covered in the *Leeds Mercury, Norfolk Standard, East Anglian Daily Times, Glasgow Evening Citizen, Glasgow Evening Times* and the *Dundee Advertiser.*

During the 1895-96 session there was a joint meeting with the Cambridge Union. The undergraduates dominated the opening speeches on a motion that competition has proved detrimental to morality. It was just carried. The minutes reported that the debate had run over time and many people had left. The society later debated whether all the learned professions should be open to women. This was defeated, as was a motion questioning free trade policies in face of the agricultural depression.

A motion on whether MPs should be paid was debated and defeated, as too was a motion on blood sports. There were debates on the unpaid magistracy, the Education Bill , trade unions, breach of promise and capital punishment. Most of the debates around this time were political. The society voted against capital punishment, slightly surprisingly in those times, and also against trade unionism. An interesting subject for debate in November 1896 was 'that the parties to the Triple Alliance and China and Japan would be better allies for this country than France and Russia'. The Triple Alliance comprised Germany, Austria-Hungary and Italy. The motion was just defeated and it would be interesting to know what was said. There were certainly a few in politics who foresaw that an *entente* with France, which was to be consummated a few years later, could eventually lead to war with Germany.

There were several motions in the 1897-98 session about the state of the nation's general wellbeing, such as whether it was so luxurious as to lead to effeminacy, and if the excess of athleticism was beyond all reasonable bounds. The missing words in motions like these were 'for people like us'. The members of the society appeared not to take into account, or have any comprehension of, what life was like for the working classes. A motion supporting women's suffrage was carried only with the casting vote of chairman Charles Martineau. The termination of the Unionist compact on Ireland was debated and defeated. The majority of the political *cognoscenti* thought that Ireland should not be given away, nor indeed should any other part of the Empire.

In the 1898-99 session there were debates on an alliance with the USA and an established church. The society also gave its support to a protectorate over Egypt. The subject of the impromptu debate was that

Birmingham was the worst governed city in England. It was lost, not surprisingly, by 26 votes to two. The society also debated whether the Liberal Party was defunct and that was defeated by 14 votes to nine. Perhaps the framers of the motion could see into the future. With the rise of the Labour Party, which did not obviously appear to represent the future at that time, there was only to be one more Liberal government The Independent Labour Party fielded 28 candidates in the 1895 election and the Social Democratic Federation four. All were defeated, including Keir Hardy who lost to a Conservative in West Ham.

The Boer War had begun in 1899 and several motions addressed the issues. A motion that 'it is necessary in the interests of the British Empire that all able-bodied men should be compelled to undergo military training' was carried by a narrow margin and one can only surmise that the vote reflected the state of mind of the nation at the time. National service or anything that smacks of a standing army has never previously appealed to the British. Later in the session the subject of a joint debate with the Birmingham Central Literary Association was that absolute annexation of the Boer Republics should be avoided. A jingoist majority defeated the motion by a very wide margin of 139 votes to 27. In 1901 the society debated a motion that 'the government has not earned its present majority'. This referred, of course, to the 'khaki election' of that year. This Liberal motion was defeated by a substantial margin which again suggests that the society was, by now, irretrievably Conservative.

Queen Victoria died in January 1901 and those attending the next meeting a few days later were sent home as the debate was cancelled as a mark of respect. In March 1901 the society, jointly with the Birmingham Central Literary Association, considered the motion 'that the Sovereign's declaration against Roman Catholicism should be abolished as being opposed to religious toleration and equality, calculated to alienate the allegiance of many loyal subjects and unnecessary for the safety of the constitution'. King Edward VII had only recently succeeded his mother and would have made this declaration in his coronation oath and it was probably this that brought it to the attention of the society. One hundred years further on, this motion would almost certainly have been carried but, in 1901, it was defeated by 54 votes to 37. It is difficult to be certain whether this resulted from attachment to tradition or deep-rooted antipathy to the Roman church. The latter is much more likely in an era when religious matters loomed much larger than they do today.

The Boer War still provided issues for debate such as the replacement by the War Office of General Redvers Buller as commander-in-chief. Buller, who had won the Victoria Cross 20 years earlier, paid the price for the early setbacks in the war, some of which can be attributed to his incompetence as a commander. Neville Chamberlain, who joined the society in 1899, addressed the society for the first time in this debate, speaking in favour of the motion. He was on the winning side and Buller was condemned by a substantial majority of the society. The verdict of history is much the same.

Neville Chamberlain was 31 years old at this time. He lived with his father at Highbury, in Moseley on the outskirts of the city (the family had lived previously in Augustus Road, Edgbaston). In 1890 he had been sent to the Bahamas by his father to run an ill-starred family venture in growing sisal and this kept him away from the country until 1897. This was a character-forming experience but, when he returned home, Chamberlain felt public life was not for him. He wondered if there was room for a third Chamberlain: his half-brother Austen was already a junior minister. He was left alone at Highbury (he married relatively late in life) while Parliament sat: his father and Austen being absent in London. When he did join the debating society in 1899, it was perhaps his first hesitant step towards a career in public service. He could hardly have been unaware of the importance of public speaking if he was to succeed, but from the first his somewhat sanctimonious manner got under the skins of those who opposed him. It seems that the debating society did nothing to eliminate this unhelpful characteristic.

Neville Chamberlain became Lord Mayor of Birmingham in 1915 and when he eventually entered Parliament for the first time he was 51 years old. When he became Prime Minister in 1937 the Second World War was only two years away. The policy of appeasement of Germany will forever be linked with his name, even though he only inherited it, and he was possibly more blamed for what followed than he deserved to be.

An interesting motion in January 1902 was 'that the Liberal imperialists cannot consistently remain members of the present Liberal party'. Neville Chamberlain opened in the affirmative. The divide in the Liberal ranks between the Liberal imperialists, whose somewhat diffident leader was the former Prime Minister Lord Rosebery, with his key supporters being Asquith and Sir Edward Grey, and the Little Englanders led at this time by Harcourt and Morley, never really came to a head as other issues loomed larger when the party regained power in 1906. Chamberlain must have spoken persuasively, as the motion was carried by a substantial majority. Ironically, his father was soon to tear the Conservative party apart with his advocacy of imperial preference and thus pave the way for the Liberal's massive majority.

Another joint debate with the Cambridge Union in November 1902 was on a motion that the present government does not deserve the confidence of the country. It was defeated by 63 votes to 23. Arthur Balfour had taken over as Prime Minister, succeeding his uncle Lord Salisbury, and the society voted solidly Conservative on this issue as it did on several other political motions. Neville Chamberlain joined the committee at the AGM in October 1902. In December that same year, two impromptu debates were held on the same evening. This decision to debate a second motion was a result of the speakers drying up on the first which was that 'the growth of large towns is a national danger and calls for remedial and preventative legislation'. The second motion was 'that the influence of public speaking is greater than that of literature'.

It is instructive to look at the general tenor of motions for debate in this era. Many of them were of the 'things are going to the dogs' type and this reflects an innate conservatism of the members and their belief that the world in its present state was as good as it gets, or at least it was for them. But the 'golden summer' of Edwardian England was not to last. Many other motions on political matters or literature required that the members were well informed or they would not be able to contribute. A new type of motion, on generalities rather than specifics, was appearing increasingly at this time. This sort of 'make of it what you will' motion may give rein to wit, but the debate itself can lack focus. Over the years that followed they were referred to as 'abstract' motions by their critics, of whom the author is one.

Neville Chamberlain led again on a motion in February 1903 that 'the society heartily approves of the financial and commercial policy of the present government as exemplified in the new taxes, the Sugar Bounties Convention and the shipping subsidies, and believes that the same principles may with advantage be still further extended'. This is the sort of motion that is debated by a society which considers the governance of the nation to be a serious business. It is not difficult to conclude that Neville Chamberlain himself chose this motion which would, of course, allow him to shine. In March there was yet another motion that the government had forfeited the confidence of the country. The Conservative majority within the society combined to defeat this motion by a solid margin, but the fact is that the government had already began its slide towards overwhelming electoral defeat in 1906.

CHAPTER 11

The Wright brothers made their first powered flight in North Carolina in 1903 but the US Army decided that flying machines would have no military value. By 1905 motor cars were appearing on the roads and soon outnumbered ponies and traps. The Liberals won an overwhelming victory in the general election of January 1906. They were led by Henry Campbell-Bannerman but, because of ill health, he handed over to Herbert Asquith in 1908. Throughout the year there were frequent demonstrations by women suffragists.

In 1903 the society, in a semi-public debate, considered a motion that 'the adoption of a system of preferential tariffs with the colonies is essential to the maintenance of complete imperial unity'. Imperial preference was Joseph Chamberlain's last great cause and it tore the Conservative party to pieces. Commitment to free trade had been embedded deep in the national psyche since the repeal of the Corn Law in 1846. Chamberlain had now managed to split both the two main parties in his lifetime, a rare achievement. The country soon decided that food prices might rise and they would have none of it. The result for the Conservatives was the disastrous election of 1906. The motion was carried. Neville Chamberlain did not lead in this debate and the minutes leave us with no indication whether he played a prominent part.

Neville Chamberlain led for the negative against a motion that, in the best interests of the country, universal naval and military training should be adopted. He carried the day. He also figured prominently in another debate soon afterwards, speaking for 'the adoption of a tariff system of reciprocal preferential duties would be in the interests of the agricultural industry and of the rural population at home, and would tend by increased commercial interests, to still further strengthen the union between the colonies and the mother country'. This was little more than a reprise of the motion debated a year previously, but tariff reform was still the big issue of the day and filial duty as much as his own views would have decided Chamberlain's position on this issue.

At this time there was a society debate that 'in the opinion of this society, women should be admitted to the professions of holy orders and of the law, and to membership of the Birmingham and Edgbaston Debating Society'.

This was carried. The inclusion of the sensitive issue of female membership of the society in a motion for debate, rather than as an amendment to the rules of the society, meant that it was no more than a test of opinion. Argument within the society on this issue was to run and run for another century.

There was a combined debate with Oxford Union in February 1905 on a motion that 'it is essential for the welfare of the country that a Liberal government be forthwith put into power'. The motion was defeated. The political facts of life were that the Conservatives were nearing defeat and Joseph Chamberlain's campaign for imperial preference and tariff reform was one of the main reasons. Nonetheless, the vote against the motion by 39 to 21 indicates that the society's political position was right of centre.

A list of members with addresses, published in 1905, indicates that two-thirds of the society's membership lived in Edgbaston. A number of other addresses listed in Newhall Street, Corporation Street, Bennett's Hill, Temple Row, Colmore Row and New Street, suggest that business addresses were being used for correspondence. Addresses in outlying areas such as Handsworth, Sutton Coldfield, Barnt Green and Walsall are also noticeable. By now there were automobiles on the streets and horse-drawn taxis and omnibuses were easier to come by.

In November 1905 there was a debate that the entrance by this country into any offensive and defensive alliance with a foreign power is contrary to its traditional policy and to its best interests. Neville Chamberlain opened for the negative and carried the day. But perhaps the affirmative had right on its side. It is possible to claim that alliances - particularly the *Entente Cordiale* with France - drew the nation into the 1914-18 war. History repeated itself when Neville Chamberlain was Prime Minister, 24 years later, and an alliance with Poland led to a declaration of war on Germany in 1939.

The motions debated were serious political issues at this time. For example, the society considered whether German foreign and colonial policy was directly and designedly antagonistic to British interests in spite of German assurances to the contrary. The society decided it was. A motion that the newly elected Liberal government was worthy of the confidence of the nation was defeated. It was agreed in another debate that Joseph Chamberlain's fiscal policies would not solve unemployment. The society also decided that the verdict of the 1906 general election had been obtained by a 'misdirection of the jury'.

Joseph Chamberlain suffered a stroke in 1906 and that ended the political career of the city's greatest fighting politician. Nonetheless, his loyal Birmingham supporters returned him unopposed to Parliament in

1910. He was to die in July 1914, only a month before the Great War began and be buried at the Key Hill Cemetery with many other famous 'brummies'. He was a charismatic, ambitious, domineering and hugely talented man who left an indelible mark on his adopted city.

A motion that the society welcomed the increase in Labour representation (29 MPs) in the House of Commons after the 1906 General Election was defeated. A combined debate with BCLA considered a motion that 'the policy of the government, as put out in the King's speech, is worthy of confidence'. This too was defeated. As the 1906-07 session got underway, the society disapproved of the policy of HM's Government with reference to trade unions. It then defeated a motion that the adoption of socialism was the only solution of existing social evils. The society didn't want to know when it came to a motion on the enfranchisement of women. Significantly for the future, the society defeated a motion that the power of the House of Lords to alter radically bills passed by the Commons was a constitutional defect. All this suggests that the society had all but taken the Conservative whip!

Before a joint debate with the Cambridge Union in December 1907 the continuance of the annual summer outing, which had been a feature of the life of the society almost since it was founded, was reviewed. It involved travelling by train to an outlying town, a visit to its main attractions and dinner in a public house followed by a speech or two before returning to Birmingham. Times had moved on and motor vehicles had changed everything. People could travel more freely and an organised outing had less appeal than hitherto. There had been several previous attempts to end the summer outing and this time it was finally achieved. Having dealt with that, the meeting then want on to defeat overwhelmingly a motion that the marriage contract should be dissoluble by mutual consent.

In March 1907 the society debated that the government's attitude towards the vital interests of the British people was reprehensible. This was lost only because of the president's casting vote. With visitors included in the count, the motion was carried. This was an arrogantly worded motion - the members of the society would almost inevitably equate the interests of the British people's as being coincidental with their own. It is one of the least helpful characteristics of the Conservative party that it thinks that any electoral defeat can only be attributed to a temporary bout of voter insanity. The society began to display similar characteristics. It defeated any suggestion of curtailment of the powers of the House of Lords by 43 votes to 37. It then attributed all social reform during the period of modern party government to the Conservative party. However, some moderation was shown when it defeated a motion in 1908 that the policy of the government, as set out in the King's speech, is unworthy of the confidence of the country.

Generally, much of the debating in this era was on matters of national importance. The report of the committee itself admits that the Conservative line was being upheld on most issues. When Neville Chamberlain again moved the motion that the present government was undeserving of the confidence of the country, it was carried by a wide margin. Another less serious and more congenial motion which he put forward successfully was that businessmen make better rulers than lawyers. These were exciting political times and few then would have realised that they were witnessing the last and perhaps the greatest of Liberal governments. The quickened political pulse of the nation may have boosted attendances at debates. Although such things are only recognised with hindsight, this was a golden period for the society.

In a notice of a meeting in December 1909 the rules for an impromptu debate were clearly laid down. This merely confirmed the procedure, already mentioned in this narrative, which had been followed for the last 20 years. The notice stated that: 'The opener on each side will speak for ten minutes, other speakers for not more than five minutes each. The names of the other speakers will be drawn from a hat as the debate proceeds, but only such members as have previously consented will be liable to be called upon to speak.' What was not mentioned, but had always been the practice, was that those whose names were drawn were required to speak alternately for or against the motion.

CHAPTER 12

*Lloyd George introduced his 'people's budget' in 1909 and this led to two general elections and the Parliament Act of 1910 which curtailed the power of the House of Lords. Edward VII died in 1910 and was succeeded by George V. The **Titanic** hit an iceberg and sank in 1912. Ulster's determined resistance to Home Rule brought danger of civil war.*

Neville Chamberlain himself was now past his fortieth birthday and only on the threshold of his career in local government. The national politician had not yet emerged. He became president of the society in 1909 and, whilst recognised as a man of importance, he was not the most assiduous attendee at society debates. He gave the usual valedictory address when he retired as president on 'human development under natural selection'. There was a debate in 1910 on a motion that the growing military and naval preparations of Germany were a menace to this country. It was defeated, and the minutes of the meeting were confirmed and signed by Neville Chamberlain. This resonates down the years to 1938 and Munich.

National politics in 1909 to 1911 were dominated by the events that led to the Parliament Act which curtailed the powers of the House of Lords. In October 1909 the Lords threw out Lloyd George's budget, which included the introduction of death duties, breaking every understood precedent that the money bills of a democratically elected government should be allowed to pass. Two general elections followed in 1910 and, when threatened with the creation of 500 Liberal peers, the Lords gave way. To today's generation the government unquestionably had right on its side and it is hard to understand the situation as it was then. The Reform Bills passed in the nineteenth century had taken the nation towards democracy, but there was still some way to go. The Unionist peers believed in the aristocratic settlement and the rights of property - or put otherwise, those with a greater stake in the nation should have a bigger say about how it was governed. Not surprisingly, the debating society had several discussions on the matter and almost always returned anti-government verdicts. This was to be expected, but it suggests that the society as a whole was incapable of detachment and being able to overcome its own Conservative prejudices. Nor, one might add, were the Peers of the Realm.

In 1910 a motion debated was that the action of the House of Lords in rejecting the Finance Bill has been justified by the results of the General Election. This was carried. The fact was that the Liberal government's landslide majority of 1906 was a high water mark that could not be sustained and it still had a reduced but working majority with the support of Irish MPs. An election result can often be interpreted in a number of ways, but it requires blinkers to believe that the voters (only a minority of the population) backed the Conservative opposition. The matter was debated again only two months later in a well-attended joint meeting with the Birmingham Central Literary Association. The motion was lost narrowly this time. The society, and certainly the BCLA, were beginning to recognise that the Liberals' battle against the power of the Lords was probably a just one.

When a second General Election was called in 1910, the motion for the society's debate was that the appeal to electors is unjustifiable at this present juncture and is a violation of the spirit of free government. This was an absurdly prejudiced motion that deserved defeat, but was carried. However, the pendulum began to swing. The society debated that the conduct of the government in recommending the use of the royal prerogative to create peers in order to overcome the resistance of the House of Lords was an outrage on the constitution. This was defeated. Another motion applauding the emphatic expression by the country of its renewed confidence in HM's ministry was carried and this suggests that opinion within the society had at last moved in favour of the Parliament Act.

In April 1910, a joint debate was held with the University of Birmingham Debating Society in the latter's Medical Theatre. Three other societies took part: the Birmingham and Midland Institute Literary and Debating Society, the YMCA Literary and Debating Society, and the Edgbaston Ladies' Literary and Debating Society. Neville Chamberlain, who was also president of the university's debating society, was in the chair for the final time. The motion was that some form of parliamentary referendum, other than that of a general election, is desirable. This was carried.

A motion was discussed in March 1911 that the interests of the nation required that steps should be taken to eliminate the unfit. It was carried comfortably. One can hardly imagine a subject like this being debated in the twenty-first century. However, a debating society does not govern the country and it can indulge itself in debates that lead nowhere and change nothing. As it was still not the practice to minute what was said in debates, it will never be known what arguments were put forward.

The other big political issue in the run up to the 1914-18 war was Ireland. Home rule was still an issue and was not regarded as inevitable, and the Protestant majority in Ulster wanted no part of it. The latter were prepared to take their case to the point of civil war and the declaration that 'Ulster will fight and Ulster will be right' had been first coined by Lord Randolph Churchill. But in the mouths of Unionist politicians it was tantamount to treason. The society debated that Ulster activists were to be deplored. The majority thought otherwise. Soon afterwards, the society returned to the subject and debated that 'in view of the provisions of the Home Rule Bill, the methods of the Ulster agitators are unjustifiable and the approval of them by the Unionist leaders is unworthy of a great party'. This was defeated, almost inevitably, taking into account the climate of opinion in the society. However, the phrase 'Ulster agitators' was hardly conciliatory.

A motion that the franchise should include every adult male was lost. The Reform Bill of 1884 did not enfranchise all males and nor was it anywhere near to doing so. It was interesting that the debating society, a reasonably minded cross-section of well-informed men, did not want universal suffrage. Great Britain was not even a full democracy in 1918 as another ten years would pass before women aged between 21 and 30 were enfranchised. The idea that only the intelligentsia should vote and that the masses, if allowed to do so, would support a government advocating confiscatory socialism, was deeply embedded in the psyche of the enfranchised minority. Their attitude was summed up by a debate in 1912 on the motion that the establishment of socialism, eliminating the hope of gain and fear of poverty, would destroy the mainspring of human progress.

In March 1912 the society decided by a wide margin that it had no confidence in the present government. On more domestic matters, Sunday opening of theatres and places of amusement was decisively defeated, as was the introduction of a minimum wage. There was support for divorce reform and for co-partnership rather than socialism to remedy industrial unrest. In all these years, the average attendance was above 50.

A telegram was sent to the stricken Joseph Chamberlain in September 1913. The wording was 'The Birmingham and Edgbaston Debating Society assembled at its annual meeting and dinner recalls with pleasure that it is now 50 years since you, the most distinguished of its presidents, delivered the presidential address. The society desires to tender its sincere good wishes and to assure you of its lasting regard.' The reply to the telegram was 'Many thanks for your kind message. I remember with great pleasure my association with your society and wish you many more years of prosperity.'

The society debated in October that the Home Rule Bill should not be proceeded with further without an appeal to the country. In carrying this motion, the society showed little understanding of how representative government worked. There was absolutely no reason why the Liberal government should have to appeal to the country for a further mandate before implementing a policy that it had supported for 30 years. Generally, the anti-government motions put forward by the solid Conservative phalanx in the society came thick and fast. A little enlightenment showed through when women's suffrage was debated again and opinion swung in favour.

CHAPTER 13

The assassination of Archduke Franx Ferdinand and his wife led to Austria's ultimatum to Serbia and the 1914-18 War. Britain lost 750,000 of its young men and twice that number were wounded. The Russian Revolution took place in 1917 and Mussolini formed the Italian Fascist party in 1919. Women over 30 were given the vote in 1918 and hemlines began to rise from the floor for the first time.

The Great War had started by the time that the new session began in September 1914. There was a vote of good wishes to some half dozen members of the society who had volunteered for military service. It was agreed that they and others who volunteered should be kept on the members' list. To begin with, motions at this time did not address war issues. This changed a little with debates on what constitutes a *casus belli* and press censorship. But there was plenty of discussion of other subjects.

In March 1915 there was a motion debated that the war had destroyed international socialism. The motion was only just defeated. Whilst the widespread advance of socialism itself was a consequence of the war, the motion almost certainly referred to the Socialist International. When the crunch came, workers of the world did not unite to prevent the war. The committee's report for the 1914-15 session reported that nearly 40 members were serving in the war and, so far, two of them had been killed. The annual dinner was suspended, but otherwise the society continued to meet.

The society debated, in November 1915, whether some change in the mode of government, taking into account the present position of the country, was needed. The Liberal government had prosecuted the war until May 1915 when the failure at Gallipoli led to a government reconstruction with Lloyd George taking over as Minister of Munitions and Conservative leaders joining the Cabinet.

Neville Chamberlain was sent a letter congratulating him on being elected Lord Mayor of Birmingham in 1915. It is interesting that Chamberlain was in his late forties by this stage in his political career and he was still to be elected to Parliament. It is certain that no-one would have recognised that here was a future prime minister. But it has to be said that future prime ministers are often difficult to spot even when they already hold high office in a government.

By 1916 it was clear that the war was not preventing the society from meeting. Many younger men were in the army by now, but conscription had not yet been introduced. Nonetheless, the numbers attending debates were slowly being depleted. It was interesting that motions were increasingly becoming philosophic and abstract. Examples of this included 'that the sentimental side of man's nature exposes him to great danger', 'that lawyers are undesirable as statesmen' or 'that the craving for novelty is more harmful than beneficial'.

In March 1916 the president expressed sympathy to S M Slater, a former president (1902-03), on the death of his wife in a Zeppelin raid. With only 1,400 or so people in Britain being killed by air ship bombing raids during the entire war, few of them reaching as far as Birmingham, this was an unlucky death to say the least. Only a month earlier, the society had debated that a public demand for air reprisals is desirable.

The next session began in October 1916 when the Battle of the Somme had been raging for over three months. The society, after discussing the existence of ghosts, debated what was becoming a key wartime issue 'that the dislocation of commerce has been unnecessarily increased and the successful prosecution of the war hampered by the neglect to mobilise the whole nation'. The motion was lost, but the general feeling of drift was to bring Asquith's premiership to an end in December with Lloyd George replacing him. Interestingly, the latter had been the target in a number of hostile motions debated by the society since 1909: the people's budget, the Parliament Act and the Marconi scandal. However, the coalition formed by Lloyd George was Unionist dominated whilst many Liberals followed Asquith into opposition. The society, nonetheless, would have approved these changes. The voters of the nation were not consulted.

In January 1917 Lloyd George appointed Neville Chamberlain as director-general of National Services, primarily because of a recommendation from the latter's half-brother Austen. The society's president Richard Willes wrote an effusive letter of congratulation to Chamberlain, to which the latter replied warmly. As things turned out, Chamberlain, who was to prove a fine departmental minister in time, was not a success in this, his first government office. Lloyd George, with a keen interest in phrenology, was heard, after their first meeting, to say that Chamberlain had the wrong shaped head. The two men were never going to be compatible. Lloyd George had charm in abundance, but little probity:

a combination that would not have endeared him to Chamberlain. Lloyd George, some time afterwards, said the director-general's job had required a man of exceptional gifts, not rigid competency. Chamberlain resigned in August 1917 and decided to enter Parliament. With his connections, finding a candidacy in the Ladywood division of Birmingham was no great problem.

In February 1917 a motion for debate was that 'in any country, the contact of races varying in colour, religion and ideals, is an evil'. To describe such contact as 'evil' rather than merely 'undesirable' seems a little over the top. The motion was narrowly defeated. The society, in March 1917, chose as a motion that 'the economic and industrial burdens resulting from the war will justify a revision of the trade policy of this country, so as to discriminate against the manufactures of our present opponents'. This was carried narrowly, but perhaps not altogether surprisingly. Birmingham was doing well out of the war and manufacturers would not have welcomed competition from a defeated Germany afterwards, or at any time. The cry that 'Germany must pay' was soon to be heard and the economic consequences of this and of the Treaty of Versailles were not to be understood until much later. At the end of the year the society debated that all's fair in love and war. This could hardly be described as a profound matter and no doubt it allowed the members an opportunity for humour.

The society, in February 1918, decided somewhat optimistically that a League of Nations would tend to ensure the permanent peace of the world. The idea of forming a League of Nations was one of the Fourteen Points, a declaration of US war aims, announced to Congress by President Woodrow Wilson in January. It attracted worldwide enthusiasm from the public, but less from the governments of the Allies or the Central Powers. The war at this time was far from won and, what is more, it did not look like it was being won. There were still nine more months to go before its sudden and rather unexpected end. The Fourteen Points turned out to be little more than the basis for Armistice discussions.

The session which began in October 1918 debated whether a minimum wage and the right to work was an entitlement of all, and if the government should continue to exercise its control over individuals in the interests of achieving social and national ideals. These somewhat socialist motions were lost. On 20th November, little more than a week after the Armistice, the society debated that the prevalence of intellectual anarchy necessitates the control by the state of the public expression of individual opinion. In a sparsely attended meeting, the motion found, reassuringly to those who believe in free speech, only two supporters.

In December 1918 the society decided that a general election at the present time was not necessary. This referred of course, to the *Coupon Election* in which Lloyd George endorsed the coalition Liberals who supported him and not those others still loyal to Asquith. The governing coalition won by a wide margin but, with the results declared, it had become predominantly a Unionist (Conservative) party. In February 1919 Lord's Day observance was debated. The forces of conservatism won the day and emphasised the preference for a quiet and contemplative Sunday. Churchgoing mattered in those days, but there is no doubt that, in the movement to change the British Sunday which took another seventy years to achieve its aim, the government lagged behind public opinion. Extending the franchise to women was also debated in February 1919, particularly taking into account their war work. This motion was lost, but Parliament had already decided otherwise.

In March the society gave its support to the League of Nations and decided in another debate that enemy aliens should be kept out of the country for ten years, and that those already here were responsible for industrial unrest. At this time, the recent war appeared to be the result of foreign entanglements that might better have been avoided. Bolshevism now had taken over in Russia and was a force to be reckoned with in defeated Germany. The governing classes of Britain saw it as a dangerous foreign contamination. Their overriding wish was to get back to the 'normality' of 1914.

Another interesting motion which was debated in April 1919 jointly with Birmingham Central Literary Association was that 'following the analogy of the League of Nations to enforce peace, this house advocates that labour and capital be deprived of their respective weapons of the strike and the lock-out, and that compulsory arbitration be substituted therefore under the auspices of a *League of Industries*.' This sort of naïve idea has been with us throughout the twentieth century. It was a fashionable idea at the time when it became apparent that the strife of war would be followed by the strife of peace. It is easy to understand the post-war yearning then for normality or tranquillity, but politics are never tranquil.

In October 1919 the annual dinner was held again after an interval of five years. 21 attended, including Neville Chamberlain who was now an MP. The dinner was held at the Grand Hotel, in the centre of Birmingham, which was still the venue for debates. One of the first debates in the session was that government by businessmen is the only effective means of preserving the prosperity of this country. The society showed some maturity by rejecting this motion. It was said that the government's supporters after the 1918 General Election consisted of hard-faced men who looked as though they had done well out of the war. Their political attitudes were hard-nosed and their excesses had to be held back in the decade that followed by one of their own, the moderate Stanley Baldwin.

In November the society rejected a motion that capital be taxed. A month later it considered whether it regretted the increasing activity of women. This was also rejected, but not by a wide margin. With the vote being conceded, in 1918, to women over thirty, the emancipation of their sex was happening apace. The streak of male chauvinism that this aroused was a not unexpected reaction.

CHAPTER 14

Hemlines continued to rise in the early 1920s and the Catholic church described modern fashions as 'scandalous and utterly incompatible with a woman's dignity.' The Irish Treaty is signed, but the exclusion of the six counties brought civil war. The Conservative party meeting at the Carlton Club ended Lloyd George's six years as prime minister. Andrew Bonar Law, and then Stanley Baldwin, took office, but Labour took office after the 1923 general election with Liberal support. A year later the Conservatives returned to power with Neville Chamberlain as Minister of Health and Winston Churchill as Chancellor of the Exchequer. The General Strike lasted nine days in 1926. The age of talking pictures began with Al Jolson in **The Jazz Singer,** *but Charlie Chaplin said that they were a gimmick that wouldn't last. Labour was returned to office in 1929 and the Wall Street stock market crash came in October.*

In January 1920 the matter of smoking during debates was considered again. What previously had been the understanding was that smoking was permitted but not when women were present at meetings. The liberated young post-war women were smoking cigarettes and it was fashionable to do so. The previous rule no longer made sense, but the vote (17 to eleven) was far from overwhelming. At the same meeting the subject for debate was that it would be to the advantage of the country if a Labour government were to be in power. This was defeated narrowly. Later in the month a motion that the coalmines be nationalised was also lost by a narrow margin.

Other motions in the session concerned Ireland and alcoholic liquor, two of the burning issues of the time. The usual joint debate with the Birmingham Central Literary Association discussed the Treaty of Versailles. The motion for its revision was lost. At this time the French were losing British sympathy as a result of their hard attitude towards defeated Germany. This debate was held in the YMCA lecture hall in Corporation Street. In the new session, which started in September 1920, the house approved of the government's policies on Ireland. This policy was to fight the IRA. The Government of Ireland Act proposed Parliaments in Dublin and Belfast with limited power, reduced Irish representation at Westminster and a Council of Ireland to reinforce unity. If it was enough to satisfy Ulsterman and the debating society, it pleased nobody else.

In April 1920 the committee was faced with the fact that 101 members were in arrears with their subscriptions. It was agreed that the secretary should no longer send them notices of debates and that they be omitted from the list of members. Whilst this situation appears reprehensible, the disruptive effect of the 1914-18 war had changed the routines of life for so many people. Some of those who came back from the war may not have come back to the debating society. Generally, the secretary on behalf of the committee wrote to the widows of former presidents who had died of old age. The records suggest that their deaths were usually 20 years or more after their terms of office and this gives the clue that they were in the early fifties when president. Some of the earlier presidents died 40 to 50 years later and, taking into account the shorter life expectancy then, it is certain that many of them were still in their twenties when they held office. It is interesting that there was nothing surprising about this in those early Victorian days whereas, in the period between the wars, the young were considered frivolous and not ready for responsibility. It was the era of the middle-aged and youth did not re-assert itself until the 1960s.

In February 1921 there was an attempt to allow members who left early to have their votes recorded provided that at least two speakers from each side had been heard. This was defeated by a wide margin. Trade Unions were debated twice and the house did not support what were hostile motions on either occasion. In March the society, jointly with the BCLA, debated whether the coalition government was unworthy of the confidence of the country. The 1918 General Election had left the coalition with over 500 MPs, mostly Conservatives, Not unexpectedly the solidly pro-government members of the society defeated the motion.

The Irish question was again debated in January 1922 with the British government being supported. In February 1922 the society debated that it would not approve an alliance with France. This was lost only on the casting vote of the chairman. It was felt at this time that the network of alliances between nations had been a root cause of the 1914-18 war. In the same month the society debated whether the time is ripe for a general election. This was defeated but was prescient. The Carlton Club meeting at which the Conservative party decided to fight under its own banner and not Lloyd George's was still eight months away.

In a joint debate with the BCLA in March 1922 the motion was that the meeting views with apprehension the present trend of trade unionism. It was carried by 92 votes to five. The fear of trade unionism at this time was strong, but the near unanimity of the vote suggests the society was overwhelmingly Conservative. With the alternative government emerging to be Labour rather than Liberal, the society closed its Conservative ranks but for a few maverick exceptions.

In October 1922 the AGM and dinner were held as usual at the beginning of the session. Some financial matters were agreed: specifically that anyone who had been a member for ten years could become a life member for five guineas. There was a graded scale that allowed those who had been in membership longer to pay even less. Those who had been members for 25 years or more were asked to pay two guineas. This is a not unusual expedient for organisations experiencing some financial problems. At this time the annual subscription was seven shillings and sixpence. The extent to which such offers are bargains depends on the anticipated level of inflation in the years to come and the age of the beneficiary. As it happens, the rate of inflation between the wars was very low indeed. In this instance, however, the objective was to retain a connection with senior members of the society who might otherwise resign. The membership was 214 at this time and 134 of them were eligible for these concessions.

The longstanding relationship with the BCLA led to a cricket match being organised between it and the debating society. The latter won by five wickets. The committee report at end of session referred to the game and also re-stated that the main objective of the society was to train members in the art of clear thinking and lucid expression of thought.

In November 1922 the society debated and carried a motion approving the return of party politics. This was soon after the famous Carlton Club meeting on 19th October at which the Conservatives decided to fight the next election as an independent party. This was not with the approval of the coalition-minded Austen Chamberlain who was leader at the time. Lloyd George resigned immediately and a Conservative ministry led by Andrew Bonar Law took over until an election was held. Austen Chamberlain had backed the wrong horse and, though he was still to be Foreign Secretary (1924–29), the highest office eluded him. Neville Chamberlain was appointed Postmaster-General and the society's letter of congratulation to him was politely acknowledged. However, he had barely he got his feet under the table when he was promoted to be Minister of Health, a bigger job then than now, as it included responsibility for housing, old-age pensions, the poor law and health insurance.

A motion for debate that socialism was a moral perversion was only just defeated. Whether the Labour party of the time was socialist in tooth and claw is open to doubt, but Conservatives probably chose to believe that it was. In the General Election of November 1922 Labour won 142 seats which made it the official opposition. In terms of votes cast, the party did much better than that, but the British electoral system can throw up unreflective results in three-party contests. The Liberals were split between those loyal to Asquith and the National Liberals led by Lloyd George.

In January 1923 the society approved the conduct of the Italian *Fascisti* by a relatively wide margin. It then supported the French occupation of the Ruhr. Two months later the motion was that, in a joint debate with the BCLA, in the context of the French occupation, that the British should pursue its own policy regardless of the *Entente*. This was defeated.

Bonar Law's ill health led to his resignation and Stanley Baldwin took over as Prime Minister. In April 1923 he promoted Neville Chamberlain to the Treasury and there was another letter of congratulation from the society. Baldwin made a declaration in favour of a protective tariff in November as being the only way to overcome unemployment. The society debated this declaration and gave its support, for what it was worth, to the Prime Minister. However, Baldwin felt honour bound to take such a fundamental change to the country, even though he had an unassailable majority. In the General Election which followed, the nation's attachment to free trade and 'cheap food' was too strong and, even though the Conservatives still finished up with the most seats, the first Labour government took office with Liberal support in January 1924. Ramsay MacDonald became Prime Minister. The first concerns of the nation about a Bolshevist takeover began to subside and astonishingly, in March, the society approved the programme of the government. There were subsequent motions which suggest that the first Labour government had attracted some sympathy, possibly stemming from relief that things were not as bad as first feared. Nonetheless, the Labour minority government was bound to be defeated before long and so it was. The Conservatives returned to power in 1924 and Winston Churchill, rejoining the party he had left 20 year previously, was appointed Chancellor of the Exchequer. Neville Chamberlain again became Minister of Health. He could probably have had the Exchequer if he had pressed for it, but he told Baldwin he would prefer Health. Chamberlain was to prove a very good departmental minister and, by the next election in 1929, he and not Churchill was unquestionably the next in line to succeed Baldwin.

In November 1925 the society decided that the country was better off without a British *Fascisti*. Its attitude on this had changed since the debate in 1923. In March 1926 the society considered whether an equal and universal parliamentary franchise was undesirable. This was lost, but not by an overwhelming majority. The commitment within the society to universal democracy was still only skin deep. The General Strike took place in May 1926 and this influenced the choice of motion in October that drastic alteration in the law relating to trade unions was urgently necessary. The motion was only just carried.

When five new members were admitted in 1927, the voting process involved shells instead of the usual beans. The approval - or blackballing - of new members was done using a ballot box with 'yes' and 'no' drawers. Questions asked about why there were no longer any beans after 74 years were dealt with humorously by the chairman of the meeting, Thomas Kennedy, who was to become president in 1929, and the incident was reported in the local paper. Kennedy also proposed in a committee meeting in October 1927 that ladies should be invited to join the society. After some talk on the matter, it was agreed that the secretary should find a date for a resolution to be discussed. However, in January 1928, the matter was looked at again in order to consider whether the proposal should be debated or dealt with as a constitutional amendment. It was decided to debate the issue at the next meeting instead of the agreed motion. The precise wording decided upon was 'that the committee be instructed to frame a rule permitting the election of ladies as members, and to submit it for adoption at a subsequent meeting of the society this session'. Thomas Kennedy led for the affirmative, but he was unable to carry the meeting. The motion was defeated by 31 votes to 13.

At the next meeting the society dealt with the motion postponed to make way for the debate on female membership. It was that the middle classes were the backbone of England and, unsurprisingly, it was carried by 18 votes to eight. Next, the society debated and agreed that the present (the 1920s) was the most vulgar epoch in history - a somewhat grumpy middle-aged verdict on the times. The pink end of the membership's political spectrum had its chance with motions proposing the abolition of the public schools and then, a month later, the House of Lords. Both propositions were soundly defeated. Generally the motions debated indicate the temper of the times, for example: world peace can only be secured by disarmament - lost narrowly; the death penalty for murder should be abolished - overwhelmingly defeated; newspapers abuse their licence - just lost; the desirability of a united European economy - just lost.

The meetings of the society, which had been at the Grand Hotel for a long time, were transferred in October 1929 to the Assembly Room at the Chamber of Commerce in New Street. The AGM in 1930 was held at the

Grand Hotel, but ordinary meetings continued at the Chamber of Commerce - a presumed economy measure in bad economic times. There were still well over 200 members at this time. Annual dinners continued to take place and Neville Chamberlain attended in 1929. His party's defeat in the General Election in June had no doubt freed up his time.

A proposal, after amendment, was agreed at a meeting in 1930 that 'with a view to maintaining the character and traditions of this society its procedure where not specifically regulated by the existing laws shall follow our established customs and usages and that any important departure from such established customs and usages shall receive the sanction of a general meeting'. This is a lawyer's drafting and the lack of any punctuation does not help to make it intelligible. When this proposal had been discussed thoroughly at the meeting (and had been agreed by a relatively narrow majority) and there had been further argument about the times of meetings, there was no time left for the scheduled debate.

The society debated in November 1930 whether dictatorship was essential to the future wellbeing of the country. That this was defeated and that the margin (25 votes to 17) was narrow should come as no surprise to those familiar with the history of the times. The Wall Street crash had been followed by an ever deepening depression and a number of people were losing faith in democracy itself. There was a yearning for a strong man to sort out the nation. Hitler's day had not yet come, but it had been noticed by members of the society, like everyone else, that Mussolini had made the Italian trains run on time.

In January 1931 the society predictably disapproved of gambling and, at the next meeting, overwhelmingly defeated a motion that prison should be reformatory rather than punitive. At this time the middle classes of the country were perhaps more homogenous in their political outlook than hitherto. They were solidly Conservative, respectable, conscientious, pompous by the standards of today, and lacking a sense of humour about anything they considered important. It was not an age for satire or parody. The older generation were dominant and anyone yet to reach middle age was not considered ready for responsibility. These attitudes persisted into the 1950s and it was not until the 1960s that everything changed.

Politics had also changed of course. Until 1918 the Conservatives had faced the Liberals in the Commons and the upper- and middle-class voters could be found on either side of the political spectrum, even though issues such as Home Rule and the powers of the House of Lords proved very divisive. When the Liberals gave way to Labour, a greater solidity took over the body politic: the country was divided between two solid phalanxes whose supporters were there to the death. In these circumstances, a relatively small shift of opinion in a general election was enough to lead to a change of government. By this time the political divide was now clearly marked out between free market capitalism and socialism, and thus it remained until the 1990s. It is a reasonable guess that members of the debating society who voted Labour between 1918 and 1997 were very much exceptions. With the advent of Tony Blair and New Labour, it is difficult to be confident about this any more.

CHAPTER 15

A national government was formed under Ramsay MacDonald in 1931 to deal with the economic crisis and most Labour MPs went into opposition, leaving the Conservatives dominant. Adolf Hitler became Chancellor of Germany in 1933. King George V died in 1936 and was succeeded by Edward VIII who abdicated before the year was out. The Spanish Civil War began in 1936. Neville Chamberlain became prime minister in 1937, succeeding Stanley Baldwin. Winston Churchill had been in the political wilderness for several years by then.

In December 1931 the society discussed whether amateurism had a deleterious effect on sport. The minutes at this time still did not include anything of the line of argument in debates and the motion was heavily defeated. It is surprising that the motion accused amateurs of having a deleterious effect when, in those times, it might just as easily been professionals who were 'in the dock'. In the two decades between the wars there remained a social gulf between amateurs and professionals. In cricket they had separate changing rooms and, at some county grounds, walked on to the pitch through separate gates. Golf professionals were not allowed in club houses and Rugby Football was an amateur game: there was no way back for those who went North to play Rugby League for money. This carried on after the 1939-45 war: the MCC touring team went by boat to South Africa in 1948 and the four amateurs - it goes without saying that these included the captain - dined at a separate table. After the war there was a period of 'shamateurism' in some games, particularly in lawn tennis, until the hypocrisy of it all was stripped away in the 1960s.

The society decided in January 1932 that its records should be entrusted to the custody of the Public Libraries Committee of the Birmingham Corporation and that is where they have remained ever since. The debate that followed in the same meeting was on disarmament being a necessary condition of the survival of civilisation. The motion was just defeated and the narrow majority indicates the high level of pacifism at this time. The society found itself deadlocked over whether ladies should be admitted to the annual dinner. The vote was 15 - 15 and the president used his casting vote to defeat the proposal. At the same meeting the society resolved to return to the Grand Hotel for its meetings and this is where they were held until well into the 1950s. The Grand in Colmore Row vied with the Midland in New Street to be the premier hotel in Birmingham's city centre.

These were difficult economic times and a National Government led by the Labour prime minister Ramsay MacDonald had been formed to deal with the crisis. Most of MacDonald's Labour supporters had refused to accept the measures considered necessary to save the nation's finances and went into opposition. They were decimated in the 1931 general election which followed with the National Government asking for, and getting, a 'doctor's mandate'. In reality it was a Conservative dominated government with MacDonald placed uncomfortably at its head, a situation reminiscent of Lloyd George's after the 1918 General Election. Any motions for debate at this time which criticised the new government were decisively defeated and this was not surprising as the political colour of the society was now overwhelmingly blue, and of a deepish dye.

The joint debate with the Birmingham Central Literary Association in March 1932 proposed that democracy, as a form of government, was a spent force. This was defeated by 35 votes to 20, but the yearning for decisive leadership - in other words for a dictator - was an undercurrent which flowed quite strongly at this time. Whether it would ever have come to anything is open to doubt. Hitler had not yet acquired power in Germany, but Mussolini's certainties had impressed some people. Sir Oswald Mosley's British Union of Fascists was active in this country. Hitler became German Chancellor in January 1933 after an inconclusive general election and, in October, the society debated that Hitlerism has been the salvation of Germany. Amongst the speakers in the affirmative was a German national invited as a guest. The motion was lost and the debate was reported in the *Hamburger Zeitung*.

The society debated in November 1933 a motion that it should favour a system of government based on fascist principles. Amongst the attendance of 48 were several members of the British Union of Fascists in the same black-shirted and jackbooted uniform worn by Hitler's *Schutzstaffeln*. They were guests and were not ejected or held up to ridicule, but their presence must have been intimidating and alien to everything the society stood for. The motion was defeated, but far from overwhelmingly. The local branch of the British Union of Fascists then proposed a joint debate a few months later. The committee made its excuses on the unconvincing grounds that its programme for the session was full.

Before Mosley formed the New Party in 1931, Michael Foot recalled of him that 'no rising star in the political firmament ever shone more brightly.

By general assent, he could have become the leader of either the Labour or the Conservative party.' Mosley entered Parliament as a Conservative in 1918 but joined the Labour party in 1923. He had to be found a constituency which he could win as a Labour candidate and, in the 1924 General Election, he contested Birmingham Ladywood. In unfavourable circumstances for his party, he lost very narrowly to Neville Chamberlain by 77 votes. He eventually won a by-election in Smethwick in 1926. Forming his new political party in 1931, even out of frustration, was a step too far. Mosley's star soon faded and, when financially supported by the German government, he became little more than a potential traitor. As it happened, the committee had tried hard to persuade Mosley to speak at the society's annual dinner in 1931.

A very distinguished member who had joined the society in 1892, Justice Henry McCardie, died in 1933. He was committed to social justice and impatient with legal purists. He was regarded as one of the great common law judges of England. Also in the same year Fitz-James Sawyer, who was president 20 years earlier in 1913, was ordained rather late in life. He wrote in to resign because of the new demands on his time. As he had joined the society in 1904, the committee allowed him life membership at the commuted fee of a guinea.

In January 1934 the society debated a motion that 'condemned and deplored the constitution of a university which openly tolerates the public expression of disloyal and unpatriotic sentiments'. The motion was lost and it refers, of course, to the Oxford Union debate in 1933 that 'this house will under no circumstances fight for king and country'. This was carried in the union by 275 votes to 153 and shockwaves reverberated round Europe. Winston Churchill called it 'an abject, squalid, shameless avowal' and some claim that the result influenced Hitler's foreign policy. The mood was lightened at the end of the session with a debate that golf was a clog upon national progress. The word 'clog' means obstruction, of course, but its usage is not common nowadays. A motion like this cannot be taken seriously and merely offers participants the opportunity for wit. It was lost.

In February of the following year the society debated that the world is a better place now than it was when it first met (in 1846). This was carried, not unexpectedly. The problem with this sort of motion is the definition of 'world'. The word is used in the abstract sense, of course, but what members of the society would have been thinking is whether it was a better place for well-to-do professional people like themselves living in Edgbaston, a very small sample of the worldwide population. The 1930s were a golden age for the middle-classes in Britain, but whether the world was a better place for the teeming masses in Africa and Asia would not have entered anyone's thinking. If there is not clear agreement amongst those present about what a motion means, a debate will lack focus.

The regular annual joint debate with the Birmingham Central Literary Association in March considered the motion that the house had no confidence in the government. It was carried by 31 votes to 30. This was a surprising result and perhaps it suggests that the participants from the literary association were not as right of the political spectrum as the members of the society. Leading for the negative was Councillor Walter Higgs, soon to become a Member of Parliament. He represented the West Birmingham constituency from 1937 to 1945. The debate was reported in detail by the *Birmingham Post*. Another future MP, Gordon Matthews, also joined the society at this time. He was to represent the marginal Meriden from 1959 to 1964. A little later Leonard Cleaver's name appeared in the records of the society. He was to become MP for Birmingham Yardley in 1959. Coincidentally, he worked for Chance Brothers which has already been mentioned in this narrative.

There were, in the 1934-35 session, a number of abstract motions debated: the first two were that 'the fool is a greater menace to society than the knave' and 'material prosperity is detrimental to character'. Abstract motions are open to wide and differing interpretations and, as a result, many of those taking part have little idea what side they are on both during and at the conclusion of the debate. Throughout this decade the society also held what it called 'smoking debates'. These were usually called at the end of the annual session and the motions were less serious. It is not quite clear why smoking should have had anything to do with the weightiness of the matters under discussion.

The society urged re-armament on the government in October 1935. This was slightly surprising as Stanley Baldwin, by now Prime Minister again, felt that the General Election earlier in the year might have been lost if the spectre of costly re-armament was part of the government's platform. When one takes into account what followed, Baldwin, a fine Englishman in every way, harmed his posthumous reputation by not coming clean on the need for re-armament. It is easy to demand that politicians should 'trust the people' but it doesn't always pay electoral dividends. The National Government's majority was very large and Labour was in the doldrums so, whatever Baldwin and the National Government had stood for, the 1935 election would have been very difficult to lose.

However, in January 1936, the society decided that the National Government had forfeited its confidence. Why this should have been so is not clear from the records. The government's big majority was, in truth, a Conservative majority, and one would have expected it to have the support of the society. The 'National' name lingered on out of respect to the National Liberal and National Labour MPs still in its ranks. Thus things remained until 1945.

King George V died in January 1936 and, three weeks later, the president of the society referred to 'the great loss that had been sustained by the whole world and especially the British Empire' - a pardonable exaggeration. Proceedings were then adjourned. The King was widely respected and the monarchy had been brought closer to the people as a consequence of his Christmas radio broadcasts. In his last New Year's Honours List was included a knighthood for Patrick Hannon MP, a member of the society but a very infrequent attender.

Censorship of the press was discussed in March 1936 yet again 'under the control of a statutory non-political body'. The motion was convincingly lost, but it is interesting that this subject was being raised repeatedly in the 1930s. The feeling that democracy was decadent and that the dictatorships were better disciplined and efficient is one that could be encountered in those days. It is one of the less attractive aspects of the reactionary right that it incessantly returns to the need for press censorship. In the same month the house considered whether it should 'condone the recent acts and declarations of the German government as affording the best opportunity of negotiating a lasting peace in Europe'. The members voted 18 - 14 in favour but, with the visitors included, the vote was 22 - 24 against. The visitors clearly had more sense.

In October 1936 the new session opened with a debate that a combination of England *(sic)*, Germany and Italy was required to resist the spread of communism in Europe. The absence of France in this grouping had everything to do with the fact that its government was now the Popular Front led by Leon Blum. Nonetheless, alignment with Germany and Italy was an unappetising prospect and the motion was solidly defeated. Later in the same month the motion for debate was that the restoration to Germany of her colonial territories would be welcomed. This was only narrowly defeated.

The abdication crisis at the end of the year was not debated at all by the society. Because of the discreet silence maintained by the Press, the British people as a whole, including the members of the debating society, only became aware of the crisis by the time it was virtually over. It is part of the *raison d'être* of a debating society that it debates political and social issues as they happen. Once the 'file is closed', there is little more to be said on the matter and it is time to move on to something else that is exercising the minds of the members or the nation. At this time over half the households in the country did not have a daily newspaper and were even less likely to have had a wireless (as a radio was then called). Even for the better informed, there was nothing like the sort of media scrum providing the up-to-the-minute news that we have today. In the 1930s the country could wake up and find that it had lost its king or was at war with little forewarning that it was about to happen.

The society rejected compulsory military service by a margin of two to one in March 1937. This suggests that members of the society were still unaware of what was going to engulf them in a little over two years time. Nonetheless, conscription was something that had never appealed to the liberty-minded British and it was a divisive issue in 1916, the only time in the nation's history that it had been introduced so far. It would take the outbreak of another war to persuade the country to accept it again.

The joint debate with Birmingham Central Literary Association took place at the Grand Hotel. The motion was that 'this house censures the government for its failure to give a lead in international affairs'. It was lost by 24 votes to 19. Things were not going well for the National Government. In 1936 the Hoare-Laval Pact to partition Abyssinia caused many MPs to rebel and brought objections from the Conservative grassroots and Hoare's resignation. Germany had re-occupied the Rhineland and the Spanish Civil war had broken out. The society approved non-intervention in the latter in its several debates on the subject.

When the 1937-38 session started in October there was no message of congratulation to Neville Chamberlain on becoming Prime Minister, or any record of it in the minutes. He had taken office in May which was, of course, the close season for the society and perhaps therein lies the explanation. Chamberlain was the undisputed successor to Baldwin. He was the 1924-29 Conservative government's most successful minister and was, as Chancellor of the Exchequer, the architect of the nation's economic recovery after 1931. He was a dedicated public servant with an incisive manner which brought respect, if not affection. He entered parliament in 1918, when he was in his fiftieth year, having done little notable except being Birmingham's Lord Mayor (1915-16).

Robert Rhodes James in *The British Revolution* has written of him that 'his disdain for the bulk of his political contemporaries was not wholly unmerited, nor his contempt for the vapid temporisings which are the stock-in-trade of most politicians, and which were particularly evident in the inter-war parliaments. But it was his most conspicuous political defect that he could not and did not conceal these emotions. Furthermore, he appeared to have a sadistic pleasure in exposing ignorance, laziness and shallow thinking. Although a limited man, he towered over most of his colleagues, and not least for his application. His shyness was a major element in his failure to make those casual friendships which are so essential to popularity in the House of Commons. It was his place of business, never his home. His only recorded visit to the Smoking Room was artificial, embarrassing, and not successful. He was too quick to pass hostile judgment. But, if he was intolerant - as he was - it can be argued that he had much to be intolerant about. His mastery of the House of Commons was complete. His weapons were immense application, mastery of his subject, and a freezing belligerence which his opponents found profoundly intimidating.'

His shyness, lack of geniality or *fausse bonhomie* - which today would be considered as a serious handicap in politics or social life - were less obvious in the more formal and reserved mode of behaviour around the turn of the century. Nonetheless, Chamberlain in private was a much warmer man altogether than his public *persona* suggests. History has not judged him kindly and probably never will.

Towards the end of 1937 the society debated the fall in the birth rate, hire purchase, the decay of capitalism and the repatriation of Spanish refugees. At this time the membership had fallen a little to 200, but the debates were well attended with the average rising from 42 to 63. In March 1938 the society solidly defeated a motion that it had no confidence in the Prime Minister's foreign policy. Anthony Eden had recently resigned as Foreign Secretary and this was discussed, but the society supported Chamberlain. Soon afterwards, the society were guests of Birmingham Central Literary Association and the motion was that it was 'the duty of the British government to take necessary measures to safeguard the independence of Czechoslovakia and other similarly situated nations'. This was lost and the society at this time clearly felt, echoing Chamberlain's own words, that Czechoslovakia was 'a far away country of which we know little'.

There was also talk at this time whether the annual cricket match against the Birmingham Central Literary Association ought to be replaced by a golf or tennis match. Clearly the problem was getting 22 cricketers together in the same place and time. The great majority of the members opted for golf and a match was played at the Moseley Golf Club in June 1939. The society lost by seven matches to five. There had also been a medal golf tournament for members of the society and the BCLA in 1938. Cricket matches between the two organisations had been played in 1933 and 1935.

When the society started the new session in October 1938 Chamberlain had been to see Hitler in Munich. The society president announced, amid applause from the members, that a telegram had been sent to Chamberlain. The message was 'Members and friends of the Birmingham and Edgbaston Debating Society assembled at the 92nd annual meeting desire to tender recognition of the stupendous efforts of their ex-president and member, the Prime Minister.' Chamberlain politely acknowledged these good wishes as always, also by telegram. At the next meeting of the society the government's policy towards Czechoslovakia was approved yet again. No shift of opinion could be detected within the society and this was reflected in the country generally. In early 1939 the session ended with a series of predominantly political debates.

At a committee meeting in December 1938 Peter Osler raised, with justification, a complaint about the increasing tendency of some members to read speeches from manuscript. The secretary was instructed to circulate a notice reminding members that it was contrary to the traditions of the society for speeches, whether from the table or the floor of the house, to be read.

CHAPTER 16

War against Germany was declared in 1939. France fell in 1940 and Winston Churchill succeeded Neville Chamberlain as prime minister. The BEF only just escaped from Dunkirk. The Battle of Britain was won in 1940 and Germany invaded Russia in the Summer of 1941. The Japanese attack on Pearl Harbour in December 1941 brought the USA into the war and ensured eventual victory for the Allies.

The next session would have been due to start in September 1939 as usual but, in the meantime, war had been declared. Because Armageddon was expected at any time, all debating society activity ceased. However, when it was realised that it was to be a period of 'phoney war', two debates were organised in January 1940 and another two in February. One of motions was that the country should declare war on Russia. This was lost. The committee's attitude at this time was that it should keep the society ticking over with an occasional meeting. The last meeting of the session was in April 1940 and when the society met again in October, things were very different. Winston Churchill had replaced Neville Chamberlain as Prime Minister, the BEF had escaped from Dunkirk, France had fallen and the Battle of Britain had removed some of the anxieties about invasion. The first debate of the session was that the house favours a policy of reprisals against the enemy. The vote was tied six to six and the chairman of the meeting, W E Marston, use his casting vote to carry the motion. The society also discussed whether meetings should be held during a weekday lunch hour or on a Saturday afternoon. The point had been raised that some members might be unable to afford lunch. The matter was left to the committee which decided that both were to be tried. One consequence of the war was that the president, Herbert Wilkes, a solicitor, had an extended three-year term of office from 1938 to 1941, when he was succeeded by Marston.

In the 1940-41 session there were only two meetings, both held in the lunch hour. The society was clearly struggling because of the war. Neville Chamberlain was stricken by illness in July 1940 and died in November, but there is nothing in the minutes about it. He must have been a disillusioned man seeing all that he believed in trampled underfoot by the German dictator, but his belief in ultimate victory remained undiminished to the end, even if he was never to see it.

BIRMINGHAM AND EDGBASTON DEBATING SOCIETY.

SESSION 1908-1909.

President.
ALBERT LUCAS.

Ex-President.
BERTRAM O. PEMBERTON.

Vice-President.
NEVILLE CHAMBERLAIN.

Committee.

G. J. G. BOTTELEY.	SIWARD JAMES.	BERNARD PARKER.	L. ARTHUR SMITH.
A. A. CADDICK.	J. BERNARD MARSHALL.	A. R. RANN.	GARDNER TYNDALL.
J. LAWRENCE HAWKES.	A. D. MATHEWS.	P. E. SANDLANDS.	RICHARD A. WILLES.

Hon. Auditors.
A. W. HEATON.
F. H. LAMPLUGH.

Hon. Treasurer.
COUNCILLOR E. M. RUDLAND,
14 TEMPLE STREET (Tel. Central 1901).

Hon. Secretary.
FITZ-JAMES SAWYER,
NEWHALL STREET.

18th February, 1909.

DEAR SIR,

A Meeting of this Society will be held at the **GRAND HOTEL, on WEDNESDAY NEXT, FEBRUARY 24th,** when the subject for discussion will be:

"That the present Government is undeserving of the Confidence of the Country."

Affirmative.
MR. NEVILLE CHAMBERLAIN.

Negative.
MR. WILLIAM C. CAMM.

The Chair will be taken at 7-30 p.m.

The presence of ladies and other friends is invited.

At a Meeting held on February 10th, the Resolution discussed was "That the attitude of the Confederates to the Unionist Free-Fooders is an abuse of Party Methods and a Disgrace to English Political Life." The voting was:—For the Resolution, Members, 7; Members and Visitors, 9. Against the Resolution, Members, 11; Members and Visitors, 17.

Yours faithfully,

FITZ-JAMES SAWYER,

Hon. Secretary.

Notices of meetings were always printed until the advent of the Internet, This one in 1909 shows that Neville Chamberlain, then a vice-president, was leading in the debate.

able during the term of office of the last Administration it was that their executive work was weak and incapable. When Mr. Chamberlain accused the Government of refusing to put the law in operation he did not mean the ordinary law, but exceptional law—that which was intended by what was known as the Crimes Act. It was coercion the Unionists for some reason or other were hankering after.

During the three years the Liberal party had been in office they would have reduced the National Debt at the end of this financial year by something like forty millions. It was difficult to know why Mr. Chamberlain should have objected to British capital being invested abroad, because it was admitted by all the great economists that where there was an investment abroad of capital it meant an increase in the exports of the country. It was through exports that capital got invested abroad, and he always understood the great object of Tariff Reform was to promote exports. In the field of legislation the Government had, he claimed, statutes which tended to the improvement of the great masses of the people. A brisk discussion ensued, the affirmative side of the proposition being upheld by Councillor Murray, Councillor Rudland, and Messrs. G. Bown and Marshall Freeman, whilst for the negative the speakers were Messrs. H. Jackson, S. D. Lewis, Frank Roscoe, and the Rev. George Clarke.

The voting resulted as follows:—For the affirmative (members), 35; against (members), 17. For the affirmative (members and visitors), 70; against (members and visitors), 3

FEBRUARY 25, 1909.

BIRMINGHAM DEBATING SOCIETY.

THE POLICY OF THE GOVERNMENT.

SPEECH BY MR. NEVILLE CHAMBERLAIN

"That the present Government is undeserving of the confidence of the country" was the subject for discussion at a meeting of the Birmingham and Edgbaston Debating Society, held last night, in the Grand Hotel, Birmingham. Dr. A. Lucas presided over a large attendance.

Mr. Neville Chamberlain, who took the affirmative, pointed out that the resolution was in effect a vote of censure on the Government, and that it was drafted on such broad lines as to throw open for debate the whole field of the Government's policy in all its aspects. The Government, he reminded them, came into office with the highest hopes, the biggest promises, and the most powerful Parliamentary majority any of them could recollect, and yet, within three years they had fallen in the estimation of the country with a rapidity and completeness that were equally unparalleled. It was true the opportunities afforded the country of reducing the Government's majority in the House of Commons had not been sufficiently numerous to allow Unionists to make much impression on that somewhat motley phalanx, but bye-election after bye-election had had a certain moral influence on the Government, and the Liberal party were now in a somewhat more chastened spirit than before. With an iteration which had become almost monotonous, the bye-elections had told the same story, and as one

---

seat after another had gone, or Liberal majorities had been reduced to a vanishing point, the conviction must have been borne in upon the Government that they had lost the confidence of the country. There was one point on which the Government could fairly congratulate themselves, and for which no Unionist would refuse them credit. He referred, of course, to their foreign policy. And then, as regarded national defence, Unionists were willing to concede that, although there was much to criticise in the Government's attitude in relation thereto, such solemn promises and explicit assurances had been received from the Prime Minister that it would be ungenerous to doubt he would keep them like an honourable man. But when he left the two subjects of foreign policy and national defence what a lamentable record they had to examine! It was curious to mark the course of the procedure adopted by the Government. He remembered that when he was a boy at school they used to hear about a three-headed monster in the shape of a dog, called Cerberus, but it had been left for the Government to introduce another kind of monster—a cat, which the Government, like the housemaid in the story, blamed for what things were broken or missing. To put the political situation in the form of a mathematical expression—"What the cat is to the housemaid, so is the House of Lords to the Liberal party." Referring to the debate on the Address, Mr. Chamberlain said Mr. Ponsonby and his friends had allowed themselves to be taken in by the Prime Minister and the President of the Board of Trade, by believing that they meant business when they fulminated against the House of Lords. Had they come to Unionists, Mr. Ponsonby and his friends would have been told nothing of the kind was intended. He (Mr. Chamberlain) did not propose to go into the details of the withdrawn or rejected Education and Licensing Bills, because he might be told that was all past and done with, but he thought that even now, at the eleventh hour, if the Government would turn over a new leaf and show they had statesmanlike and practical proposals for dealing with the problems of the day, the people would be willing to give them a new lease of life. Turning next to the Old-age Pensions Bill, the speaker, while approving the provision made for the aged poor, pointed out that the bill had been introduced with no adequate means of meeting the cost thrown on the British taxpayer. With regard to Ireland, Mr. Chamberlain said enough had been uttered during the debate going on in Parliament on this subject to show that during the administration of the Government, and especially since the egregious Mr. Birrell had been in office, many parts of that country had gone from bad to worse. The whole administration of justice had been demoralised, and outrages had increased both in number and daring and violence. And yet Mr. Birrell refused to put in force the powers at his hand which would diminish crime and bring peace and security to Ireland. As a consequence of the repeal of the Arms Act by the Liberal Government it was less safe to go about some parts of Ireland than it was in Central Africa. He ventured to say that, if there were no other count in the indictment against the Government what had taken place in Ireland was sufficient to justify them in voting for the resolution. Unionist extravagance used to be a favourite theme of Liberal oratory, yet they (the Liberals) had now got things to such a pass that, with a falling trade and a declining revenue, they found themselves face to face with an expenditure far greater than anything the Unionists had to encounter. The "Rake's Progress" began in 1906, when the Government gave away £4,000,000, every penny of which would have been paid by the foreigner, by abolishing the coal tax. In 1907 Mr. Asquith said any scheme of old age pensions must be one to which all classes must make a just and adequate contribution, and yet in 1908 when he brought in the bill without calculating the cost he deprived himself of 3½ millions of revenue by taking off the sugar duty. With regard to the problem of unemployment, Mr. Chamberlain asserted that by their reckless speeches and Socialistic legislation the Government had driven a large amount of capital out of the country and, in that way, directly contributed to the amount of unemployment. And while thus contributing to the spread of unemployment the Government on the other hand, had done nothing appreciably to mitigate it. They had one great opportunity at the time of the conference with the colonial Premiers, but they preferred to bang, bolt, and bar the door in the face of the colonies.

The local Press covered debates in detail.

Birmingham and Edgbaston Debating
Society.

CONCERNING FAME.

A VALEDICTORY ADDRESS

BY

GARDNER TYNDALL,

PRESIDENT FOR THE SESSION,

1904-1905.

Delivered at the Annual Meeting of the Society,
held on the 11th of October, 1905, and printed at the
request of the Members.

HUDSON & SON, EDMUND STREET AND LIVERY STREET,
BIRMINGHAM.

*Valedictory addresses by outgoing presidents were printed and stored
with the society's records in Birmingham's Central Library.*

The centenary dinner in 1946. Standing (left to right): G F Boston (president Cambridge Union), Peter Osler (vice-president elect), Judge R A Willes, L F Daniels (honorary secretary) and R F Brown (president Oxford Union). Seated: Alderman A S Giles (Lord Mayor, Birmingham), Howard Heaton (president), Gordon Matthews (president elect) and Dr E W Barnes (Lord Bishop of Birmingham).

Presentation in 2000 to the 'father of the house' Ken Wilkinson by president Peter Barnett. Standing behind (left to right) are Reg Willsher, Geoffrey Crofts, Tony Grazier, Bill Caswell, Richard Tudor, Philip Gretton and Ian Marshall.

| *Walter Higgs* | *Leonard Cleaver* | *Chris Baker* | *Tim Ryan* |

| *Dr Anthony Joseph* | *Conrad Charles* | *Geoffrey Burcher* | *Bill Caswell* |

| *Tony Grazier* | *Professor John Hilbourne* | *James Fergus* | *John Masterton* |

William Moyle   *Geoffrey Oakley*   *Raymond Burton*   *Tony Ridgway*

Roger Stone   *Kenneth Wilkinson*   *Richard Tudor*   *Tony Houghton*

Ian Marshall   *Stephen Gilmore*   *Donald Wasdell*   *Reg Willsher*

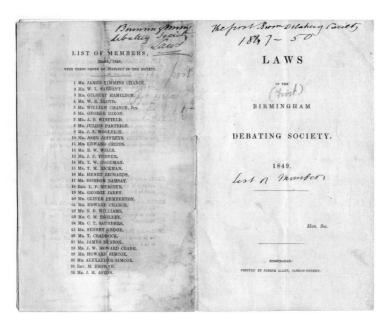

The front page of the laws and the list of members of the first Birmingham Debating Society in 1849.

James Barwell speaking in March 1947 while the honorary secretary, Francis Bromilow, takes minutes.

Spencer Comley seconding a motion in March 1947. Seated is C. V. Hackett of the Birmingham Central Literary Association.

1

Session 1896-97

<u>28ᵗʰ October 1896</u>

A dinner was held at the Grand Hotel at Birmingham on this date to celebrate the Jubilee of the Society (the Edgbaston Debating Society having been founded on the 8ᵗʰ October 1846)

The Right Honorable Joseph Chamberlain M.P. LL.D, D.C.L (the President) took the Chair at 7 o'clock p.m.

The following were present:-

Original members of the Edg Debating Society

Surgeon Major H. M. Greenhow   E. Payton

B. S¹ J Attwood Mathews   J. C. Barlow

Councillor R. J. Martineau   and   E. K. Blyth

Past Presidents of the Society

Watts W. J.	(Edg Socy 1854-55)		
Saunders C. J.	(1857-58)	Bunce J. J.	(1858-59)
Johnson G. J.	(1859-60)	Mathews C. E.	(1860-61)
Harris Wᵐ	(1864-65)	Caddick Alfᵈ	(1869-70)
Lowe T. C.	(1873-74)	Park Archibald	(1874-75)
Ryland W. H.	(1875-76)	Harrison C A.	(1877-78)
Lowe J. W.	(1879-80)	Malins Edwᵈ	(1880-81)
Lee J. G.	(1881-82)	Maccarthy Rev E. M.	(1882-83)
Osler A. C.	(1884-85)	Madden E. M.	(1885-86)
Carter W. J.	(1886-87)	Carter A. H.	(1887-88)
Lee E. Henry	(1888-89)	Eales Henry	(1890-91)
Lloyd Jordan	(1891-92)	Crosskey Cecil	(1892-93)
Clarke Rev J G	(1893-94)	Williams E. Bickerton	(1894-95)

The first page of the report on the golden jubilee dinner in 1896 which lists the founder members and past presidents who attended.

The society held two meetings again in 1941-42 starting at 6pm. Germany had invaded the Soviet Union and the society responded by debating whether there should be an immediate second front. Only 18 months earlier (see above), it had debated whether Britain should declare war on Russia! Unsurprisingly, nearly all of the debates in these years were war-related, but the Beveridge Report was an exception: it was debated on a Saturday afternoon in January 1943. Another Saturday afternoon meeting in March, jointly with the Birmingham Central Literary Association, discussed a motion that private ownership and control in industry is detrimental to the peace of the world. Speaking against was Walter Higgs MP. The motion was defeated narrowly which suggests that socialist ideas were taking hold at this time. Gordon Matthews, the honorary treasurer at this time, had to relinquish the office when he joined the Royal Navy.

The president in 1942-43 was Alexander Comley, a coal merchant, mine owner and brick manufacturer, who dressed immaculately and always with a flower in his buttonhole. In a debate some time later on a motion that the house prefers a public house education to a public school one, he spoke for ten minutes in Latin! His son Spencer was to be president of the society twice (1956-57 and 1967-68). In November 1943 the house defeated a motion favouring a Soviet Union style of government in the UK. It is a surprise that such a motion should have been proposed at all, but many people then were ignorant of the appalling tyranny that the Soviet Union actually was. At the time, it was regarded as a brave ally. A motion more worthy of debate was that the post-war prosperity of Germany was essential to the future peace of Europe. It was narrowly defeated.

The society got by with three meetings in 1944, but there was now a widespread belief that the war was being won and life would soon get back to normal. There was nothing to suggest that the society thought it did not have a future. New members were still joining the society including Sir Peter Bennett MP in 1945. He represented the Edgbaston constituency for the Conservatives until he became a peer.

The society debated whether motor cars and aeroplanes should be abolished in March 1945, a motion which allowed scope for tongue-in-cheek nonsense and it is unlikely that those speaking in the affirmative believed in the case they were making. At this time of war, there was little or no civil aviation, except internally in the USA, and members of the society would only have thought of aircraft as weapons of war. The motion, unsurprisingly, was overwhelmingly defeated.

In April 1945 with the war nearing its end and victory assured, the society debated, jointly with the Birmingham Central Literary Association, whether Neville Chamberlain's journey to Munich was justified. The motion was carried surprisingly. But then one must consider that Chamberlain was one of the society's own and perhaps the collective viewpoint was that, without having the benefit of hindsight about what sort of man Hitler was, Chamberlain had done all he could.

CHAPTER 17

Labour won the 1945 general election and Clement Attlee became prime minister. The post-war years involved economic difficulties with shortages and rationing. Europe was divided by the 'iron curtain' into two opposing camps. 1948 brought the Berlin airlift and the founding of the state of Israel. The Korean War started in 1949. The second BBC television transmitter opened in the Midlands in 1949 and life was never the same again.

The 1945 General Election brought Labour to power with a big majority. The election had been called soon after VE Day and the result surprised many at the time. At this time of year, of course, the debating society is not in session and, as a result, there was a noticeable absence of debates about the electoral issues. It would also not have passed without comment that two members of the society contested the Edgbaston constituency: Sir Peter Bennett (Conservative) defeated Corbyn Barrow (Labour). The former had entered Parliament in 1940 and was soon after appointed Parliamentary Secretary, Ministry of Labour and National Service. Gordon Matthews fought the Labour stronghold of Deritend.

Spencer Comley was a particularly active secretary in the immediate post-war years. Both he and his predecessor J F Daniels made efforts to build up the status of annual dinners by issuing invitations to the great and the good, including A.P. Herbert and Viscount Samuel, and some of them, not unexpectedly, declined politely. George Bernard Shaw, for example, pointed out that he was approaching his 90th birthday!

The first debate after the war was on the atomic bomb and the majority decided that its use against Japan had been 'injudicious'. This was an understated word for such a cataclysmic event. Mixed opinions on this most dramatic of military decisions certainly began to form in the months that followed, but the society probably delivered its own verdict too early. In November 1945 there was a joint debate at the Grand Hotel with the Oxford Union attended by 80 members and undergraduates and it seems that things were rapidly getting back to normal. One debate in December 1945 that presaged much that was to follow was 'that the time had come for women to be admitted to the privileges of membership of the society'. The motion was lost.

The society was also in discussions with the BBC about whether it would be possible to broadcast debates on the radio. It was pointed out by the broadcasting technicians that speakers would have to come to a single microphone and that this might interfere with the flow of debate. Discussions lingered on for two more years, but there was nothing in the papers to suggest that it was a serious possibility. A BBC internal briefing paper referred to the society having been formed in 1846 by schoolboys!

When the 1945-46 session opened the society began to focus its attention on the centenary a year hence. A dinner and speeches were planned and it took place a year later, on 23rd October 1946, at the Grand Hotel. Amongst the invited guests were the Bishop of Birmingham, the Lord Mayor, Judge R A Willes and the presidents of the Oxford and Cambridge Unions. The main speeches following dinner were those of the bishop and the judge. Both talked about Neville Chamberlain's place in the history of the society and that understanding was needed of the difficulties he faced at Munich. The evening was not on the lavish scale of the golden jubilee celebrations in 1896, but that could hardly have been expected in those frugal times. The 'top table' comprised officers of the society and their guests who all wore evening dress (white tie and tails) with the notable exception of the judge who came in a dinner jacket, which is probably what most of the members might have worn that evening.

There was clearly some concern in the next few months about the level of support for the society and the president told the committee that he was sending letters to a number of local organisations including the Law Students Society, the Chartered Accountants Students Society, the Young Conservatives, the Co-operative Society, the Commercial College, King Edward's Grammar School, the Workers' Education Association, the Young Liberal Movement and the Young Labour Party Movement, in order to make them aware of the existence of the society. There is no record of whether this produced any results. Another initiative was to bring back to life the Summer outing which had lapsed 40 years previously. The Stratford upon Avon Shakespeare Memorial Theatre was one of the venues chosen.

In November 1946 a special meeting was convened to discuss the future of the society. Gordon Matthews, the then president, read a letter from Kenneth Wood, a former president (1934-35), in which the latter urged the society to uphold its traditions and to revert as far as possible to its old practices and procedures. Wood was not against innovations as long as they were in the interests of the society. He was against guest speakers and thought that members preferred to debate amongst themselves. The president pointed to declining support and appealed for a more open door policy with regard to new members. Other members wanted a livelier and less formal atmosphere. One described it as 'sepulchral'. That there were too many abstract motions for debate was also raised. Questions were asked about the Grand Hotel as the venue for meetings. Whether cost had anything to do with this is not clear from the minutes. The Council Room of the Chamber of Commerce was suggested as alternative. The annual subscription was more than doubled at this time: from ten shillings to one guinea.

There was a proposal that women should be admitted as members. There was a show of hands and the vote was against by twelve votes to ten. Whilst a vote in favour might have forced the committee's hand, it would not have had any validity without agreement at an EGM which had been called with the appropriate period of notice. It was to be nearly another 50 years before women were accepted beyond argument as full members of the society. After the weighty issue of female membership had been discussed, but not settled of course, the society debated a frivolous motion that 'work is the curse of the drinking classes' the vote was tied with nine for and against. The president gave his casting vote against the motion.

At the 1946 AGM there was an amendment proposed to the society law which related to balloting that revised wording should include the phrase 'new members of either sex'. This was regarded by some as an oblique way of securing the right to membership for women, but it was carried nonetheless. However, certain members argued, with justification, that the acceptance of ladies as members merited a special debate and that it should not be introduced 'by stealth' in the guise of an amendment to a rule. It is no surprise that the amendment was to be subsequently challenged on two occasions on the grounds that it conflicted with other society laws. On this issue, the society found itself in a position that was not unique then and continued to be a matter of concern for clubs and societies of all sorts right up to the present day. It never occurred to the members of a new club or society being formed in the early to mid-nineteenth century that women might have wanted to join at some indeterminate time in the future or, one might add, that they would have been enfranchised or allowed to work in the professions. As a result, rules drafted at the time did not cover such a contingency. Those who argued subsequently that, in the wording of these rules, the masculine should not be assumed to include the feminine, had the stronger case and indeed the original society laws included the word 'gentlemen' in one instance. Whilst it is better to meet such issues head on, there was nothing to suggest in the records that the amendment was introduced unconstitutionally. But the situation with which the society had been left was not watertight as laws that allowed members to blackball any applicant for membership were still in place. Blackballing is an anonymous process that does not normally require reasons to be given. A weapon had been left in the hands of those who were prepared to blackball only on the grounds of gender.

All this led to a special meeting in March 1947. It was agreed by the committee that the matter would be discussed according to the procedure followed in an ordinary debate. Nonetheless, the advance notice given meant that it was effectively an extraordinary general meeting and that the decision of the members would be conclusive. The motion was carefully drafted to prevent a single member from blackballing female candidates 'on principle'. It read 'that new members of <u>either sex</u> *(sic)* shall be elected by ballot, and no candidate for admission into the society shall be considered as elected if one-fifth of the votes given by the members present be unfavourable to his election. A candidate who has been rejected shall not be eligible during the remainder of the session in which such rejection takes place. Once again, this motion could be criticised because it avoided a straight yes or no on the issue. In any case, it could be argued that the blackballing issue had to be dealt with at the same time as, otherwise, any vote could be rendered inoperative. Nonetheless, the underlined words 'either sex' gave a clear indication of what was at stake.

It took two meetings to bring the debate to a conclusion. A grim winter had not quite ended and the battle was fought out in a poorly heated and half-lit room (because of fuel shortages and electricity cuts). Amendments and points of order, according to the report of the meeting, came 'thick and fast'. Two former presidents were in opposition. Hubert Neep, proposing, argued that the society occupied a prominent place in the life of the city and, to some extent, influenced public opinion, and that the society was 30 years out-of-date and being illogical by excluding women. Thomas Varcoe, opposing, claimed that the society was 'a man's society' in which there was an atmosphere of genuine friendship induced by male companionship. The ban was supported by 16 votes to seven. The local newspapers reported the debate under headlines such as '100-year ban on women to continue' and 'behind the times' but in reality it had only bought the anti-female lobby a limited amount of time. The matter was to be debated again in 1953 and a female member was to be elected in 1956.

Amongst other matters dealt with at that time, it was agreed that both the proposer and opposer should be allowed to sum up, but for no more than ten minutes. Previously, only the proposer summarised at the end of a debate. Another interesting suggestion was that members should be addressed, more traditionally, by their surnames. One member demanded parliamentary language. It was also proposed that meetings should start at 6.30pm rather than 7.00pm. This is one of those things that fluctuates to and fro and, in less than a decade, the decision was to be reversed.

The house considered whether it supported Sir Stafford Cripps (1889-1952) in his opposition to lengthening the skirt. The motion was defeated. Clothing coupons were part of the system of post-war rationing and the New Look of the Paris couturier, Christian Dior, was hardly likely to appeal to the ascetic President of the Board of Trade, soon to become Chancellor of the Exchequer.

In the immediate post-war period debates were well attended. For later generations too young to have lived through the immediate post-war years, their perceptions are one of a grey drabness, perhaps influenced by the old black and white films of the period. The times were austere with fuel shortages, food and clothing coupons and, to make things worse, the severe winter of 1947. It is noticeable that, in some pictures of a joint debate with the Birmingham Central Literary Association taken that year by a photographer from the local *Sunday Mercury*, listening members were seen to be well wrapped up in overcoats and scarves. This was attributable to the fuel crisis of the time and central heating was the exception rather than the rule. The pictures also show that the middle-aged and elderly predominated. The men were wearing not particularly well-fitting suits - possibly pre-war - made of heavy cloth with waistcoats or jerseys. The female guests all wore hats. Nonetheless, there were some younger men playing an active part in the society and the president, Gordon Matthews, was in his late thirties. Matthews was married to a daughter of Sir David Brooks, a former secretary and president of the society who has already been referred to in this narrative. Matthews's aspiration to become a Member of Parliament was eventually to be fulfilled twelve years later.

It was not all doom and gloom at this time and the younger generation thought it deserved a bit of fun, now that the war was over, and decided to make the best of things. Rationing and the shortages of everything remotely luxurious meant that, for the upper and middle classes particularly, there was money in the pocket needing to be spent on something. They were determined not to allow shortages and austerity to affect them too much. As a consequence, social life was vibrant. Cinemas were overflowing when a good film was showing and one had to queue outside for seats. Betting on horse racing reached unprecedented levels. League football matches drew enormous numbers of spectators which, by the standards of today, would have horrified those concerned with crowd safety. The debating society itself benefited from these phenomena and attendances were good in the immediate post-war years. All this was to change dramatically with the development of the television network.

Television was a pre-war invention, but there were few households with receivers and the service closed for seven years on the day war was declared. Until 1949 when the BBC's second transmitter opened in the Midlands, television had only been available in the South East. Compared to what the service is like today, the fare offered was not particularly palatable much of the time and there were frequent breakdowns: the placard with the words *normal service will be resumed as soon as possible* was an all too familiar sight on the small flickering screens. Nonetheless, in a few years, television was to change everyone's lives and public and social events were affected.

Another change in the lives of people, particularly for the managerial and professional classes in the 1960s, is that work became more demanding and intensive than ever it had been in the past. Until this time, 'nine to five' meant exactly that and a full lunch hour was expected. As a result, people were less exhausted at the end of the working day. When they get home nowadays, they are only too ready to settle in front of the television eating supper off a tray and the thought of going out has diminished appeal, particularly to the middle-aged.

The political battle at this time was polarised between Labour and Conservative to such an extent that there was no centre ground and the independent Liberals could muster only six MPs. (There were still some National Liberal MPs who took the Conservative whip). The more fluid and volatile composition of the electorate today was unknown then and a typical middle-class (New) Labour supporter, which one presumes must exist in abundance today, would have been a rarity in the 1940s. The debating society would still have been solidly Conservative, but socialist idealism held considerable sway in the immediate post-war years in the western world generally. In the early 1950s, however, market capitalism re-asserted itself and governments of the right began to replace those of the left.

A joint debate with the Cambridge Union in 1949 considered that 'in the opinion of this house, socialism is the road and not the barrier to communism'. The society's vote was 20 to nine in favour, but once the visiting undergraduates were taken into account, the vote was closer: 37 votes to 27.

The 102nd AGM and annual dinner that year were held at the Grand Hotel. The guests of honour were the Rt Hon Lord Pakenham, Minister of Civil Aviation, and Sir Edward Boyle, a baronet who was then president of the Oxford Union and who eventually became a Conservative MP for a Birmingham constituency and Secretary of State for Education in 1970.

In January 1950 the society debated whether the unfit should be sterilised, with Frank Blennerhassett proposing, and then that 'the weak should go to the wall' with Blennerhassett again taking a prominent part. The first of these motions was just defeated and the second, debated soon afterwards, was carried by a two-to-one margin. Blennerhassett was a barrister, later a judge, and became president of the society later that same year. His somewhat hard-line stance in these debates seems a little out of character for this likeable man. He was commissioned later by the government to advise on the working of drink driving legislation and the breathalyser and to consider whether changes in the law were needed.

In a joint debate with the Cambridge Union two months later, an undergraduate proposed that 'the nation's economy is served better by the state than by the individual'. This was massively defeated by the members 24 votes to five and by the whole house including visitors by 45 votes to 15. In the same month the society debated that capitalism was not Christian. This motion was solidly defeated and one is left with the impression that the society debated regularly about the fundamental nature of capitalism and socialism in order to avoid policy specifics that would probably have led to an even more one-sided discussion. In November 1950, a motion favouring commercial broadcasting was solidly defeated. It is not clear whether it was to co-exist with public service broadcasting or to replace it, but the result suggests a lingering distaste for certain manifestations of capitalism.

The Rt Hon Leo Amery MP was one of the guests at the 103rd AGM and annual dinner. He was by this time a veteran politician. He entered Parliament in 1911, representing the Sparkbrook constituency in Birmingham. He was First Lord of the Admiralty (1922-24), Colonial Secretary (1924-29) and Secretary of State for India (1940-45). He was a bitter critic of appeasement and played a crucial in the events leading to the resignation of Neville Chamberlain in 1940. He lost his parliamentary seat in 1945.

Kenneth Wilkinson, a quantity surveyor who was to be much involved in the post-war changes to Birmingham, had joined the society in 1950. His membership was not unbroken because of his wife's extended illness, but he did two stints as president. He was a Battle of Britain Spitfire pilot and, at the time of writing, has been the 'father of the house' for 16 years. John Freeman, a *déraciné* Irishman and insurance salesman, became a member of the society in the same year and was to be president in 1959-60. He was one of the society's characters for the next 25 years with an almost obsessive concern about eugenics and miscegenation. His views at times bordered on the eccentric. Freeman made a speech at a livery dinner in which he criticised the Church of England for owning property used for the purposes of prostitution. He was unfortunate on two counts: the Church at the time was particularly concerned about its reputation and there happened to be a journalist present. The damages were not negligible!

David Lowe was vice-president and due to become president in 1950. He was not in the best of health at the time and he advised the committee that, on doctor's orders, he could not take office. It was agreed, therefore, that he should change places in the queue with his putative successor, Frank Blennerhassett. This caused no problem to the latter and Lowe succeeded him in 1951. Although he was able to fulfil his duties as president, he never fully recovered and died young. However, his two daughters both married future presidents of the society: Richard Tudor and Ian Marshall.

CHAPTER 18

The Conservative victory in the 1951 general election brought Winston Churchill back to power. He stayed in office until 1955 when he was succeeded by Anthony Eden. George VI died in 1952 and Queen Elizabeth II came to the throne. Mount Everest was climbed for the first time in 1953 by a British expedition. Anthony Eden increased the Conservative majority in the 1955 general election.

The Conservatives led by Winston Churchill won the General Election in October 1951 by a relatively narrow margin. Later in October of the same year, the annual dinner and AGM were not held on the same day, but two weeks apart. This allowed a debate to be held on the issue of whether a measure of electoral reform would be welcomed. The house decided it would be by 21 votes to 13. With the visitors included, the vote was 32 to 15. If this seems slightly surprising now, it was less so at the time. When Churchill regained power, his majority was narrow and he attempted unsuccessfully to persuade the six Liberal MPs to join the Conservatives. The small Liberal party then was firmly in the middle of the political spectrum and bled off more votes from the Conservatives than Labour. The society probably thought that proportional representation would be a block on any resurgence of socialism. At that time the debating society, and perhaps the party itself, would not have thought for a moment that the Conservatives would be in uninterrupted power for the next 13 years.

In January 1952 the society debated that the new government was worse than the last. The Conservatives had been in power for nearly a year by then. It is no surprise that the overwhelming Conservative majority in the society did not allow this to pass. The motion was defeated by 20 votes to six and, with visitors counted in, by 25 votes to six.

King George VI died in February 1952 and the next meeting of the society was asked by the vice-president, who was in the chair that evening, to adjourn as a mark of respect. However, another member asked for a vote and the decision was eight to five in favour of an adjournment. By today's standards adjournment because of the death of a monarch might seem a little pompous and the fact that it was opposed perhaps signifies changing attitudes. Two weeks later, the society debated whether Britain should participate in a 'European Federation'. This was the first time that there was a debate about European integration and it was to be first of many. The Treaty of Rome was still five years in the future, but France's Foreign Minister, Robert Schuman, had made his visionary speech on European unity 18 months earlier in 1950. The members decided by a narrow margin that the country should participate. The members and visitors, when counted together, voted the other way.

At the AGM in October 1953 R H Hopkins was called upon to move that 'ladies have nothing to contribute to a debating society'. The motion was lost but it was only one skirmish in what was going to be a long war. At the AGM one year later, when Hopkins had just been elected president, the issue of admission of ladies as members came to the fore again. He diplomatically agreed to raise the matter with the committee. He was also asked to take up with the committee the 'appalling choice of subjects for debate'. Hopkins was a bank manager and he arranged some debates with the Midland Bank Debating Society. At a joint meeting with the Sutton Coldfield Debating Society in December 1954, the motion was that 'a happy man does not read his daily newspaper'. This somewhat fatuous subject for debate was defeated and suggests that little notice was being taken of the criticism of the choice of motions.

There was a joint debate with the Oxford Union in March 1954 on a motion that 'the policies of the western powers are ill-designed to meet the Soviet challenge'. Proposing the motion was the undergraduate Michael Heseltine, a future Conservative cabinet minister and one-time challenger for the party leadership. Leading in the negative was Eric Tranter, a member of the society who was a senior Conservative party agent in Birmingham. The motion was defeated in spite of Heseltine's efforts.

Charles Massey, a future president (1960-61), donated a cup for a schoolboys' debating competition. The first took place in November 1954 at the Imperial Hotel. The winners were King Edward's School. Charles Massey himself presented his cup after Kenneth Wood had explained why the judges had reached their decision. This competition led, in 1959, to another for schoolgirls for the Margaret Pugh Cup. The first winner was the Edgbaston Church of England College for Girls. The initiative for the latter contest came from the local education authority rather than the society. However, members were to be involved with the judging of both competitions from thereon.

In March 1955 there was a joint debate with Walsall Debating Society at the Imperial Hotel. The practice of having joint meetings with other societies was one that was followed frequently in these years. No doubt the fresh faces were welcomed. Anthony Beaumont-Dark, a future Birmingham city counsellor and Conservative MP, was elected as a member before the debate. Winston Churchill finally resigned as Prime Minister a month later and Anthony Eden, who replaced him, promptly called and won a general election.

At the AGM in October 1955 the society voted to revert the meeting time back to 7pm from 6.30pm. The outgoing president, R.H. Hopkins, thanked the officers for their support during his term and, before he could get any further, the secretary James Bowker intervened to make a statement about what he considered to be the unsatisfactory way in which officers of the society might be elected. He put forward three different conceptions of the way this should take place: (1) an automatic succession from secretary to vice-president to president; (2) the presidency and vice-presidency being in the arbitrary gift of the outgoing incumbents; and (3) that all officers should be elected at an AGM. He pointed out that the last of the three was the only constitutional procedure, but that the other two had, by custom, come to supersede it. The secretary felt that the election of officers, unlike that of committee members, was not covered properly by the rules. He requested a 14-day postponement of the AGM to allow an EGM to be held to amend the appropriate law and, at the same time, to make members aware of their right to nominate candidates for office at an AGM.

Gordon Matthews, a past president and future Conservative MP (1959-64) for the marginal Meriden constituency, seconded the secretary's proposal on grounds of principle but dissociated himself with some of the views that the belligerent Bowker, a barrister, had somewhat forcefully expressed. The argument that followed was prolonged and often heated. In the end, postponement was agreed to by 15 votes to 11.

The EGM was held only a week later. There were objections to the notice, but these related to wording: the haste with which the meeting was called, understandable in the circumstances, was apparently not a problem. The secretary sought an amendment to the law covering the election of officers which he said, though definite, was reticent. An amended law would mean that the president, vice-president, the treasurer, the secretary, the committee and two auditors, should all be elected (by ballot if necessary) at an AGM. This was carried by 15 votes to one. The meeting agreed to set up a sub-committee to examine all the laws. The adjourned AGM was held at the beginning of November and D.C. Norman was finally allowed to take office as president. Bowker, the chief protagonist in all this, did not seek re-election as honorary secretary. Very soon afterwards he became a Labour MP. When he was adopted as the candidate for what was clearly a safe Labour seat, he was scheduled to open for the affirmative on a motion critical of his party. After protesting that he dared not speak in these circumstances, he and the opposer agreed to change sides! None of this is that surprising as Bowker had always been a Liberal party member. The Liberals in those days were positioned between the two main parties but could not match the patronage that Labour was in a position to offer to an ambitious man like Bowker.

D.C. Norman had been a secretary of the society. He was a printer and owned a vintage Rolls Royce. He initiated a joint debate with the Stratford upon Avon Wranglers Society. This debate took place in the Stratford town hall and actors and actresses from the theatre company took the lead on a stage with the others sitting as an audience. Kenneth Wilkinson recalls that he led for the affirmative in the debate with the actress, Leslie Caron, speaking in support.

In December there was a joint meeting with the Midland Bank Debating Society at the Imperial Hotel. The motion was that 'it is high time that we again realised the necessity of hard work'. The motion was lost which suggests that the house thought it was working hard enough. It was probably working harder than the generation that preceded it but not anywhere near is hard as the one that followed.

It was noticeable that 1955 passed without any celebration of the date when the Birmingham and Edgbaston societies amalgamated one hundred years earlier. Understandably, one has to settle for one date or another and that decision had already been made in the previous century when the members chose to celebrate 1896 in such style. They were probably correct to do so. Unlike the Birmingham society, Edgbaston Debating Society could trace its continuous existence from 1846. It was, as explained at the beginning of this narrative, the stronger of the two societies at the time of the amalgamation and had effectively taken over the Birmingham society *en passant*.

CHAPTER 19

Anthony Eden became embroiled in the Suez crisis in 1956 which was the beginning of the end of empire and Britain's pretensions as a great power. Eden's health could not stand the strain and he was replaced by Harold Macmillan. The latter told the nation that it 'had never had it so good' and he won a large majority in the 1959 general election. 1963 was a tumultuous year. The Profumo scandal harmed the government and traditional values were being parodied in television satire programmes. US president John Kennedy was assassinated. Labour under Harold Wilson narrowly won power in the 1964 general election.

1956 will be remembered as the year of the abortive Suez invasion, but the society confirmed its commitment to the Conservatives by rejecting a motion critical of the government. The society was now meeting regularly at the Imperial Hotel, instead of the Grand. In March 1956 there was a joint debate with the Oxford Union. The motion that evening was that 'the popular press of the country is worth considerably less than the paper it is printed upon'. Frank Blennerhassett led for the negative and carried a majority of the house with him.

A month later the committee's proposed law changes were carefully considered at an EGM. The troubling issue for some was the admission of women to membership. Alexander Comley proposed, in an amendment to one of the laws, that they should be allowed to join and this was carried. This was incorrect procedure, as notice of the amendments to the committee's intended changes to the laws should have been circulated in advance of the meeting. Nonetheless, most of those present would have thought that the matter of female membership had been settled, but to have dealt with this matter in an unconstitutional way was one reason why it refused to lie down in the years ahead. The fact was that it was never going to lie down until the pro-women members had won the day, and they probably believed by now that they had done so. But at the AGM in October 1956 a motion was debated 'that this house would welcome ladies'. The honorary secretary, Dr J E Keen, led in the affirmative and John Freeman in the negative. This motion was carried by 12 votes to seven but, whilst the debate might have taken the 'temperature' on the issue, it had no constitutional validity as rule changes always require advance notice and an EGM. However, there were some who argued that a rule change was not necessary as ladies were not referred to in the original laws. This was a fallacious argument as the founding fathers of the society would have assumed that ladies were not eligible for membership and to have included this in the laws would have been to state the obvious. Sylvia Cohen, a visitor and putative candidate for membership, participated in this debate.

After the issue of lady members had been debated, there was more argument about the starting time of debates. There was no support for 6.30pm and some for 7.00pm. A compromise on 6.45pm was reached. There was also more criticism of the poor choice of motions. Spencer Comley was elected president at this meeting, succeeding D C Hopkins. Comley, at times a prickly character, was a devoted supporter of the society and, like his father, had no problems with accepting ladies as members.

However, the right to blackball candidates for membership was still a law of the society and it left a weapon in the hands of those who were irreconcilable to female members. There could be no peace on the question until that particular matter had been resolved. Whether or not influenced by Spencer Comley, the society accepted Sylvia Cohen as a member in December 1956. It is said that three members intent on blackballing her were delayed on a train! Cohen, a teacher, was the only lady member until Miss E G West was elected three years later. The latter become the society's honorary auditor in 1963. Three other ladies were admitted into the society in the next two years, but then there were none for almost a generation. One of the three was Daphne Howlett who soon afterwards stood for Parliament representing the 'Jesus Christ and His Cross' party! There was clearly no queue of ladies lining up to join the society and, as a whole, the fairer sex were far less career-minded and ambitious than their counterparts today. Sylvia Cohen was perhaps not the best person to open doors for other female members. She read her speeches which she had painstakingly written out before the meeting. There was an understanding, already referred to earlier in this narrative, that speeches (with the exception of a president's valedictory address) should not be read. By persistently doing this, Cohen's contributions to debates were less welcome than they might otherwise have been.

The Suez crisis was debated again and a motion which was critical of the government was defeated by a large majority. In January 1957 there was a joint debate with Sutton Coldfield Debating Society that 'wealth is no criterion of success'. This was carried. Another motion, that 'it is high time that women took their proper place in public affairs' was defeated. Some members, no doubt, considered that this verdict merely indicated a deep-rooted male chauvinism within the society. In March there was a joint debate with the Birmingham Labour Group. Roy Jenkins MP, on the threshold of what was to be an exceptional political career, proposed that 'this house has no confidence in the present government'. The motion was just carried by 36 votes to 33 and the result probably had much to do with the numbers that the Labour group was able to turn out.

George Craig was elected president in 1957. He was a Conservative city councillor who had also served in the RAF as a wartime intelligence officer. He was a quantity surveyor and a debater with a propensity for raising points of order. In the meetings held in December 1958 and January 1959, Donald Wasdell, John Masterton and Roger Stone were elected as members. They were all to be presidents and to play a prominent part in the future of the society, particularly when its moment of crisis arrived some twelve years later. George Craig was succeeded as president by Edwin Cutts, a senior executive at the local Mitchells & Butlers brewery. He was also to serve a second term as president (1968-69). Maynard Mitchell, a scion of the brewing family, was also a member of the society at this time. He, like Kenneth Wilkinson, had served in the RAF during the Battle of Britain. He attended debates frequently, but never spoke.

In December 1958 there was a joint debate with the Birmingham Borough Labour Party. Dennis Howell, a former football referee, Birmingham Labour MP, future Minister for Sport and eventually to be knighted, proposed that 'this house has no confidence in the government'. Reginald Eyre, a future Conservative MP for the Birmingham Hall Green constituency (later Sir Reginald Eyre and the government minister responsible for metrification in the building industry) opposed. The motion was defeated by 33 votes to 27. There was another joint meeting with the Birmingham Borough Labour Party in December 1959 and the motion was the same as before. Unfortunately, three-line whips in the Commons that night meant that neither Roy Jenkins MP nor Gordon Matthews MP were able to take part and they had to be substituted at short notice by Alec Murrie and Charles Whitehead (a future honorary secretary and president). This time the motion was carried by 31 votes to 25. This is the sort of debate in which there are no neutrals and the voting is pre-ordained. The quality of the speeches and the partisan passions are what matter. The result probably had much to do with the fact that the Labour group turned out in greater numbers than previously. It cannot be assumed, of course, that the

Birmingham and Edgbaston society was 100 percent Conservative at this time, but it was probably quite close to being so. By the time of the second debate, the Conservatives led by Harold Macmillan had won an impressive victory in the 1959 General Election.

In March 1960 a joint debate with the Oxford Union decided that the house has no confidence in the white settlers in Africa. The prime minister had made his 'wind of change' speech to a South African Parliament committed to apartheid and, although Southern Rhodesia's UDI was still five years away, the rumblings had started. The motion was carried by 24 votes to 20. This was a predictable result considering that nearly half the participants were undergraduates, most of them having little patience with white supremacist attitudes.

There was a joint debate with the Smethwick Society of Arts in November 1960. This had been organised thanks to the efforts of Edwin Cutts during his first period as president (1958-59). The motion, which was just carried, was that 'Woolworths has done more for humanity than Wordsworth'. That the choice of 'Woolworths' and 'Wordsworth' was entirely because of the alliteration is all too obvious. It is questionable whether either of them have done anything exceptional for humanity and one is left with the impression that the framers of motions were too concerned with clever phraseology. Another joint meeting, this time with the Walsall Debating Society, discussed and defeated a motion that the nation would be better off without a middle class.

In January 1961 the Birmingham Borough Labour Party again joined the society to debate whether the house had confidence in the government. The lustre of the Conservative's 1959 election victory was beginning to wear thin and a 'pay pause' (an incomes policy in all but name) called for by the government presaged troubles ahead. The house decided it had lost confidence in the government by 37 votes to 29.

The society's oldest member, William Camm, died during the 1960-61 session. He had joined the society in 1897 and was president 1915-16. Sixty-three years of continuous membership was, as far as is known, a record.

The society appeared to have started a decline in 1962. Numbers attending debates began to fall below twenty, sometimes it was as low as ten. There were joint meetings with the Smethwick and Walsall societies, but even with the visitors taken into account, there were only 22 people present on the first occasion and ten on the second. Roger Stone became honorary secretary for the first time in October 1963. The next meeting was jointly with the Birmingham Law Students Society and the society reverted to using the Grand Hotel again. The debate in November was that the house regrets the treatment of Mr Macmillan when the Profumo scandal became public. It had occurred when, John Profumo MP, the Minister for War, shared the favours of a call girl with a Russian military attaché and lied about it to the House of Commons. Profumo had also lied to Macmillan and the latter was criticised, possibly unfairly, for believing him. It was also something of a scandal on a smaller scale that only seven members and four visitors were present at the society's debate.

A meeting of the society in March 1964 attracted an attendance of eight. Then, at a joint meeting with the Erdington Debating Society, only eleven were present. In December 1964 there was a joint debate with The Debating Society of the Guild of Undergraduates from the University of Birmingham. The motion was fatuous: 'that this house does not give a damn'. Only nine members and five visitors participated. Many of the motions in this period were ill chosen and this merely accelerated the decline.

Kenneth Wilkinson was president for the first time during the 1963-64 session. Until his term of office those at the top table at the annual dinner were resplendent in white tie and tails. However, in an egalitarian move more in keeping with the times, he ruled that dinner jackets would be the dress code for everyone from thereon.

CHAPTER 20

The 'swinging sixties' brought in a pop culture, the mini-skirt and the 'permissive society'. Labour won the 1966 general election with a substantial majority but was forced to devalue the pound a year later. 1968 was a year of student unrest worldwide, particularly because of the Vietnam War. The Conservatives, under Edward Heath's leadership, won the 1970 general election and took the country into the European Common Market. But the government's economic policies were inflationary. An overtime ban by coal miners led to a three-day working week and a minority Labour government returned to power in February 1974. After Labour had won another election in October 1974, Edward Heath lost the Conservative party leadership to Margaret Thatcher.

In 1966 the society began to meet at the Law Society Committee Room in 8 Temple Street. In December of that year the author attended a society debate for the first time and became a member. Anthony Beaumont-Dark, a stockbroker, Birmingham City councillor and future MP, proposed a motion that the house should join the Common Market. The motion was lost by eight votes to seven, a result that was more surprising then than it would be now. When Beaumont-Dark became MP for the Selly Oak constituency in 1979 he was an outspoken populist who always pleased journalists by his readiness to come up with a quote on any political issue. He served on Birmingham City Council for eleven years and also on West Midlands County Council. He was knighted in 1992, after he had lost his seat in the General Election of that year, and died in 2006.

There was a joint debate with the Junior Chamber of Commerce in March 1967. After that there was a visit to Erdington for a joint meeting with the local debating society; it was unusual for the society to leave its base. The society also accepted an invitation to a joint debate with the Birmingham & Midland Institute Literary and Debating Society, and another with Bromsgrove School. More joint debates were being tried in an attempt to boost attendances, but it seems that a lot of local societies were in the same predicament. The society president, Spencer Comley, who had been elected to the office for a second time after an interval of eleven years, decreed that no apologies would be recorded in his year of office. This formal practice has always seemed to the author to be somewhat superfluous wherever one encounters it. It's difficult to convince oneself that anybody is interested, but it is an established procedure. With small attendances, the list of apologies could be potentially embarrassingly long. Only six members, for example, attended this meeting. In January 1968, the attendance dropped to five. Things were clearly going from bad to worse. At an EGM in March 1968 those present - all seven of them - considered and voted for a document that proposed the laws should be called rules, provisions for life membership should be deleted, three members were to be enough to reject a candidate for election and the fine increased to ten shillings for non-attendance after committing to lead for the affirmative and negative.

In January 1970 only the vice-president John Masterton and five other members attended and the debate did not start. Kenneth Wilkinson was president for the second time at this juncture, having previously held office in 1963-64, but none of the blame for the crisis the society faced can be laid at the door of the presidents of the time. Perhaps there was something about the 1960s: life was changing and everything had to be trendy and exciting, and leisure possibilities were opening up everywhere. For the young, there were too many alternatives to debating. Downward spirals feed on themselves and speaking to an audience of five or six soon lost its appeal to all but the society's most dedicated supporters.

Masterton became president in Autumn 1970 and inherited a very unsatisfactory situation. However, a programme was made up of four debates and an evening of three mini-debates, and the usual annual dinner. The debates were sparsely attended but the dinner, at which Masterton gave a valedictory address, attracted an attendance of 70. When the new session in October 1971 began, no successor to Masterton could be found. Anxious that the demise of the society should not happen during his watch, Masterton called a crisis dinner meeting in November (also in effect the AGM) at the Birmingham Conservative Club in Ethel Street. Arranging the dinner party was an astute move as those present could not arrive late or leave early, the bane of meetings. The future of the society was discussed and a paper submitted by Masterton was considered. This paper has not been preserved for posterity, but Masterton recalled some 35 years later that the options of placing the society in suspended animation or winding it up were included. There was agreement at the meeting that all the officers and the committee should continue for a further year. Whatever was in the president's paper did not lead to any very positive decisions. However, the dinner had been enjoyed and it was agreed that regular meetings should cease apart from an occasional dinner debate until 'such time as a more positive future for the society be envisaged.'

Nonetheless, this did not take things any further forward and the society was still in grave danger of collapsing. Five leading members - Masterton, Donald Wasdell, a past president, Tony Houghton, Bill Moyle and the secretary Roger Stone - were most involved in putting together and implementing a rescue plan based on dinner debates, building on the germ of the idea that had emerged from the dinner at the Birmingham Conservative Club nine months earlier. At the AGM in September 1972 (the society had not met since the dinner and previous AGM in November 1971), Stone volunteered to organise two dinner debates to take place in November 1972 and February 1973. A charge would be made, but a subsidy from the society's funds was agreed. Because of the crisis, John Masterton was re-affirmed as president for a third year.

The first dinner debate was held in November at the Union Club. 15 members (including the author) and eight guests attended. A vote of thanks to Roger Stone was recorded in his new capacity as dinner secretary and there is little doubt that his successful efforts to attract a good attendance to this one meeting saved the society. The motion that evening, proposed by Bill Moyle, was that 'this house supports Enoch Powell'. Powell was MP for a Wolverhampton constituency and a former Conservative cabinet minister. He was, to some extent, the champion of the unbending right and, six years earlier, he made his famous 'rivers of blood' speech at a party meeting in Birmingham which foresaw the problems that would come if unchecked immigration continued. This made him immensely popular with many sectors of the population, particularly in his home base in the Midlands, but it cost him his place in Edward Heath's shadow cabinet. He was an austere and uncompromising figure, but something of a phenomenon in his time. With the surprise Conservative victory in the 1970 general election, his star was no longer in the ascendant. Nonetheless, his aura was still enough to persuade the society to carry the motion by 13 votes to nine.

A second dinner debate followed in February, as had been agreed, and also a third in April. The next AGM was held in November 1973. By this time, and because of the special circumstances, John Masterton had served as president for three years. Tony Houghton, who took over from Masterton, suggested that, whilst there were to be only two or three dinner debates each year, the president should serve for two years. That a president should serve more than one term was not unprecedented. John Langford was the first to do so in 1871. Others who also had by this time were Joseph

Chamberlain, Herbert Wilkes, Spencer Comley, Kenneth Wilkinson and Edwin Cutts. Prior to 1855, Thomas Martineau was twice president of the Edgbaston Debating Society, as was James Timmins Chance of the second Birmingham Debating Society. It should be added that the invitation to be president for a second term has as much to do with whether a successor was waiting in the wings, or for a special reason, than as an accolade. Houghton, who succeeded Masterton, did in fact serve a second year but thereafter the procedure reverted to the predominant pattern of serving for twelve months only. Others who were to be called upon for a second term of office were Donald Wasdell, Raymond Burton, Tony Grazier and Richard Tudor. Houghton also suggested that the committee should comprise a small working group of the president, secretary, the organiser of the schools competitions (which had lapsed in the crisis period) and the treasurer. The new president was able to announce that Roger Stone and Donald Wasdell had agreed to act as secretary and treasurer respectively for a further year.

The dinner debates, having replaced the erstwhile format of ordinary meetings, began to occur increasingly frequently and with growing success, although the recovery of the society to full health was slow. Dinner debates, firstly at the Union Club and eventually at the Edgbaston Golf Club, have remained the format to this day. The one casualty of this change of policy was the society's only 'blue collar' member, H E Jakeman, an engineer who lived in Bearwood. He served on the committee in the 1960s but his eventual resignation was attributable to the introduction of what were to him effete dinners, when the previous pattern had been to start debates at 6pm so that everyone could be 'in the boozer' by nine!

The political life of the nation was in turmoil at this time. Edward Heath's Conservative government, faced with a disruptive miners' strike, went to the country in February 1974 asking 'who governs, Parliament or the unions?' In a very close election, the voters looked beyond this single issue and were influenced by rising prices which were a consequence of the government's inflationary economic policies. The Conservatives actually received more votes than Labour, but electoral geography was against them. The fact that they had lost the confidence of the country since 1970 was undeniable. Another electoral defeat later in the same year led to Heath being deposed as leader of the party and his replacement by Margaret Thatcher in 1975.

In November 1974 Tony Houghton started his second year as president by expressing a wish to revive the schools debating competition which had lapsed in the crisis times for the society. Anthony Biddle was elected secretary but, in spite of his many excellent qualities, he was not the most punctilious of minute takers. Houghton occasionally signed blank pages in the book on the understanding that the minutes would be inserted later. Houghton himself was a much appreciated character of the society. He had the ability to conjure laughter out of almost any debating situation with a *bon mot*.

In 1975 the society debated government by referendum. What had triggered this off was the referendum on the Common Market which the Labour government, led by Harold Wilson, had organised to avoid a damaging split within its own ranks on the issue. As a result, both the pro- and anti-market forces included some strange bedfellows in their ranks. The greater resources of the pro-market campaign won the day, arguably on a false prospectus which emphasised economic rather than political union, and the result would not be replicated today. The debating society, however, sensibly voted its disapproval of referenda.

The choice of Margaret Thatcher as Conservative leader led to a debate that 'the house would welcome a woman Prime Minister'. Sylvia Cohen was invited to propose this motion on the grounds that it would be an appropriate task for the 'only woman member' of the society. The other four ladies elected twenty years previously were no longer in membership. Sylvia Cohen began by asking the house to view the motion dispassionately and traced the political emancipation of women to the present day. Bill Moyle, leading for the opposition, questioned whether the female mind was given to the habit of objective decision - a line of argument that might have alienated support. It probably did as the motion was carried. What was interesting about this debate is that the minutes, for the first time ever, gave some indication of the arguments put forward by the opening speakers.

This was Cohen's swansong and her departure meant that the society had no lady members. In a confused situation, it was not clear what the rules were and perhaps the anti-female lobby sensed its opportunity. A motion put forward by a president at this time that membership should be open to women was defeated at an EGM. There is nothing in the minutes that adequately explains what the *status quo* actually was, or was believed to be. The decision in December 1956 to admit women as members, even though the procedure was faulty, had not been reversed and five ladies had been elected between 1956 and 1963. The weapon of the blackball was still in the hands of the hard-line 'antis' if they were prepared to use it. But the fact remains that no ladies had joined the society for 15 years and this requires an explanation which the minutes and the memories of the older members have failed to provide. As explained earlier in this narrative, the original rules did not refer specifically to lady members, an unthinkable prospect then, and that the society was for men only would have been considered obvious beyond doubt. That ladies be eligible for membership should, therefore, have been the subject of a decision by the members. Instead the supporters of lady members resorted to a specious argument that there was nothing in the rules to prevent it. This inevitably appeared to be an attempt to bring ladies into the society by the back door and anti-feminist members might have felt justified in using their right to blackball female applicants on the grounds of their gender alone. Whilst this could be regarded as a misuse of the blackballing procedure, it was an understandable reaction to the tactics of the other camp which, throughout, appeared to be unconvinced that it could count on a majority if it ever came to a straight vote. It appears that the pro-women lobby was attempting to pass the enabling legislation whilst not addressing the issue itself.

It is easy, however, to be judgmental on all this by twenty-first century standards. Even today, single sex clubs and societies should not, in the opinion of the author, be ruled out on the basis of some higher principle which a 'progressive' government wishes to force on them. But whether a debating society, which had allowed female guests to attend certain debates almost from the time it was founded, represented the right place to draw a line in the sand in the endless battle of the sexes seems doubtful. For the moment, however, the matter remained unresolved.

Those proposing a candidate for membership were expected to say something about him while the latter was not present. It was agreed that it would be improper, in the interests of the *amour propre* of candidates, to record in the minutes, the numbers voting for and against. This led to an interesting challenge that such a rule prohibited any record of a candidate having been elected 'unanimously'. However, the candidates for membership were, at this time, voted for *en bloc* with the agreement of the meeting. At the next meeting, Roger Stone raised a query about the choice of motions, suggesting that they were not wide enough. What he meant by 'wide' is not clear, but criticism of the choice of motions is perennial in debating societies.

There was an EGM in October 1975 at the Union Club primarily to dispose of the entrance fee for anyone under 25 years of age, and to permit a new category of country members living more than 25 miles from the city centre. By today's standards, the money involved seems trifling. A full member was to pay £4 and country members were to pay 50p. The entrance fee for the over 25 age group was also to be 50p. Another issue for the meeting was a reduction in the size of the committee to the officers and three members with four being the quorum. The committee had apparently been divided on the financial proposals. However, they were carried, but not unanimously. There was no opposition to a smaller committee.

In an interesting debate on a motion that General Franco had been right, the affirmative argued that, in this situation, a loss of democracy had to be the price paid to prevent anarchy. The motion was carried and the president Roger Stone felt constrained to advise members that new points should not be raised for the first time in summations. Stone then dealt with a number of administrative issues including that there should be two leading speakers in both the affirmative and negative, and he also stated that ladies would be welcomed to a meeting in April. Anthony Houghton took the opportunity to seek clarification on the matter of lady members and guests. He attempted to put a proposition to the meeting that the society would welcome applications for membership from ladies. The implication of this was not that ladies could not be members at the time, but that nothing was being done to encourage them to join the society. There was no support for Houghton and no motion was put to the meeting. However, Stone conceded that the society should consider the matter after proper notice on 'a later occasion'.

CHAPTER 21

Harold Wilson retired as prime minister in 1976 and Jim Callaghan replaced him. The government struggled on with Liberal support, but the 'Winter of discontent' caused by public sector union strikes cost Labour the 1979 election and brought Margaret Thatcher to power. Labour chose Michael Foot as its leader and this led to the formation of the breakaway Social Democratic Party. The Falklands War in 1982 made Margaret Thatcher unassailable in the 1983 general election.

At the January 1976 meeting Roger Stone raised some procedural points, including that heckling and interruptions should be avoided. He accepted that the latter were justified on three grounds: (1) points of order, (2) points of information, and (3) points of personal explanation. All these were to be in the president's discretion for determination. A month later, the society was asked to consider its position if a lady were to apply for membership. Tony Houghton and Bill Moyle, as immediate past president and vice-president respectively, were asked to state their views first and then others spoke. No decisions were made, of course, and Stone as president concluded matters by saying that the opinions expressed would be taken into consideration in the 'unlikely event' of an application being received. It seems that the decision to admit ladies into membership in 1956 was now being ignored as though it had never happened. The fact that no ladies had applied for membership for the last fifteen years should not have invalidated the decisions made twenty years ago.

The death penalty was debated at the February 1976 meeting and the society was in favour, but only just. In a debate in April on the motion that this house acknowledges the need for censorship, the members' vote was tied 12 - 12, and the members and visitors was tied 24 - 24, an unprecedented result in the history of the society. The president, Roger Stone, demonstrated his progressive credentials by declaring the motion lost. The total number attending that evening was 51, underlining the increasing popularity of the dinner debates.

Reginald Eyre MP, a lawyer by profession, resigned as a member of the society in February 1976. He had not attended a meeting for some time. He had been Conservative member for the Hall Green constituency since a by-election in 1965. He sat until 1987 and was knighted.

Bill Moyle succeeded Roger Stone as president at the AGM in November 1976. At the same meeting Tony Houghton raised the matter that several local societies wanted to renew the joint debates that had lapsed in the crisis years. For this meeting and more or less thereafter, the society used the Edgbaston Golf Club. Gentlemen's clubs were in decline whether in Pall Mall or provincial cities. The city's premier clubs were the Birmingham Conservative Club which had moved from Temple Row to Ethel Street and was never the same again, and the Union Club in Colmore Row which the society had used for its dinner debates in the early 1970s. The Birmingham Conservative Club was used for the society's annual dinners in the late 1960s and early 1970s. In 1974 it was renamed the Birmingham Club in the hope that this would attract a wider spectrum of members. The link with the party had always been tenuous and new members were merely asked if they upheld Conservative principles. However, its members could be relied upon to support the party financially. The club also decided to admit women members, as did many London clubs, but neither of these expedients worked and it, like the Union Club, has ceased to exist. Unlike the London clubs, Birmingham's had no evening trade to speak of and the days of a leisurely lunch hour preceded by several aperitifs and a glass of port afterwards was not something that fitted into the serious businessman's day any more.

Stone gave a valedictory address when he yielded the presidency to Moyle. This revived a tradition that had lapsed in recent years, particularly because of the crisis of survival. Stone read extracts from addresses given in 1875, 1884 and 1895. Women were invited as guests and the motion was 'that marriage is an outdated institution'. It was defeated by a comfortable margin. The valedictory addresses thereafter spluttered along for another twenty years until Tony Grazier (president 1994-96) gave what has proved to be the last.

In December 1976 the society decided that it had no confidence in the government, but only just. James Callaghan had taken over from Harold Wilson as Prime Minister. The meeting was reminded that present convention allowed speakers from the floor only three minutes. It was reported to the meeting that what little surplus funds the society had were invested, imprudently as it turned out, in Slater Walker Securities.

When the minutes of the previous meeting were read at the January 1977 meeting, Roger Stone, a stickler for correct procedure, questioned why there was reference to a 'regular' meeting of the society. The word had crept in to the minutes in recent years but was perhaps not quite the *mot just*. At the time the meeting did not agree with Stone who wanted the word 'ordinary' to be used instead. However, he eventually got his wish a few years later. At the second meeting in January 1977 the motion reprised the famous Oxford Union debate in 1933: 'that this house would not fight for Queen and country'. It was defeated by a wide margin.

The president then referred to a newspaper column in the *Birmingham Post* under the by-line John Bright. He then introduced his guest for the evening, the journalist Andrew Moncur, who wrote the column. Stone was on his feet again to suggest outside expert speakers should lead in a debate on education. He also admonished the society that all speeches should begin with 'Mr President Sir' only and no other preamble was required.

After the usual dinner at a meeting in September 1977, the invited guests were asked to withdraw while the 29 members of the society present considered a resolution put to them by Roger Stone. The latter explained that, prior to 1956, the rules of the society did not include the words 'men or women' when referring to the membership elective procedure. He added that, since 1956, only two women had formally joined the society. This was untrue: there had been five. Stone went on to say that there were no ladies on the current membership roll. This was true as Sylvia Cohen had resigned by now and that was the main reason why the matter could be raised at all: it would have been embarrassing if any decision taken might have required her expulsion. The president Bill Moyle explained that a two-thirds majority was needed to carry the resolution that the words 'men and women' should be removed from the rules. This was not watertight, as it could still be argued that the deletion did not preclude women members. There were enough votes to carry the resolution but it did not restore the *status quo ante* prior to 1956 as circumstances had now changed and the intention of the founding fathers of the society was no longer the all-important criterion. Cohen died in 1990 at the age of 89. In subsequent consideration of female membership in the years that followed, the pro-women lobby had to reverse this decision. It eventually succeeded in doing so successfully in 2000.

The meeting continued with the six guests being invited back in to the room to debate whether the house looked forward to the demise of the internal combustion engine. This was yet another example of a motion about something that was never going to happen and probably provided little more than an opportunity for amusing waffle.

Another EGM was held in January 1978. Guests were again asked to withdraw while the society considered whether candidates for membership should be required to have attended two ordinary meetings. The total membership at the time was 62, and it had doubled in the last two years, but there was concern about new members elected after attending for the first and, as it turned out, the only time. This proposal was defeated by eleven votes to ten. At the next meeting the president, Phillip Couse, referred to the difficulty of finding speakers to propose or oppose motions. He pointed out that members should not decline invitations to speak without very good reason.

In September 1978 the society was informed by Edgbaston Golf Club that major refurbishment was planned in the clubhouse. It was decided that Berrow Court, an appropriate venue considering the Chamberlain connection, should be used as a venue until the work at the club was completed in 1979. The first meeting at Berrow Court debated, after the usual AGM, the motion that the country was becoming ungovernable. Whilst the Callaghan government was on its last legs, it is surprising that this sort of 'things are going to the dogs' type of motion should be carried. In fact, the members voted 16 to eleven in favour; all six guests voted against to express a different verdict.

A motion for debate in March 1979 was another of those of which the author is critical. To debate a motion that 'the ends justify the means' allows any interpretation of its meaning and the arguments put forward in the discussion tend to confirm that. However, it is recalled by the president at the time, Donald Wasdell, that Derek Hathaway, leading in the negative, spoke particularly well in this debate. In the same month the society considered whether the trade unions were too powerful. The 'winter of discontent', when the public service unions struck and uncollected rubbish piled up in the streets, is still remembered today. Margaret Thatcher's time was about to come, but it was surprising that this motion was only just carried.

The 'Annual Ladies Evening' of the society was held at Edgbaston Golf Club in April 1979. The previous minutes had never used this title, although the last meeting of the year had previously been one at which lady guests were particularly welcome. It appears a tradition was being created with little provenance. Seventeen members attended, nearly all accompanied by their wives, and five other guests. Of the total attendance of 39, therefore, the female representation was impressively high. The motion was 'that the aim of sexual equality has been achieved' and it provoked lively debate. Roger Stone, with his usual concern for the constitutional niceties, raised a point of order whether, on ladies night, the motion was decided by a vote of all those present. Past president Philip Couse, in the chair in the absence of Donald Wasdell, declared that the members vote would decide matters. The count was ten to six in favour of the motion but, when the women guests were included, the verdict was reversed by 23 votes to 14.

In November 1979 the society debated whether it was better to be a 'three bottle man' than a total abstainer. This led to a witty and frivolous discussion, and the motion was just carried. This motion had, in fact, been debated on two previous occasions, in 1925 and 1936, with the same result. In January 1980 a motion debated was 'that the house believed the country was in decline'. Roger Stone as proposer perversely interpreted the word 'country' to mean the countryside and not the nation. After he had toured verbally through the highways and by-ways of Britain, his opponent Richard Jaffa chose to treat the motion as most would have it and spoke of the state of the nation. The president intervened at this point to insist that the motion should be interpreted as the opposer, Jaffa, represented it. Stone was invited to make a second impromptu speech in the affirmative. He did enough to win the debate narrowly. This minor *contretemps* underlines the point already made in this chapter that motions for debate should allow only one interpretation.

There was a 'Past Presidents Night' in March 1979. The minutes recorded that the president was able to welcome 'a veritable galaxy of past presidents' and singled out for particular attention was Judge Irvon Sunderland who had been in office during the war. The debate that followed considered whether newspapers were a curse. The motion was defeated as it had been when last debated in 1890. The society has always shown its commitment to a free press whenever the subject was debated.

The now annual Ladies Night in April considered whether the pleasures of anticipation are greater than those of memory. Dr Anthony Joseph, a quick-witted debater leading for the affirmative, treated the subject seriously both medically and philosophically. Ross Bellamy, leading for the negative, was a late substitute. He argued that the pleasures of memory outweighed those of unfulfilled expectations. The motion was carried comfortably. It is interesting that the guests outnumbered the members on this occasion.

In October 1979 the ever-alert Stone had questioned at the AGM whether it was in fact the 133rd rather than the 132nd for the reason that one year's AGM had not been held. The supposedly 134th AGM was held in October 1980. Roger Stone again raised the same point he had made a year ago that it was, in fact, the 133rd. He was asked to investigate the matter himself and report. At the AGM in November 1981 Roger Stone was able to report that there was some uncertainty about the enumeration of past AGMs and it was agreed that this meeting would be the 134th. Stone again raised the issue at the 1982 AGM and it was now agreed that this meeting was, in fact, the 136th. Philip Lesser appeared not to be in full agreement and it was suggested that he visit the Central Library to research the society's records. At the 1983 AGM Lesser could not recall that he should have reported back on his researches. He now found himself in a 'sub-committee' - more correctly an ad hoc committee - of three members who were asked to report back at the 1984 AGM. When the time came to report to the 1984 AGM, Lesser said that his sub-committee had not been able to establish the number of AGMs that had been held. He was thanked for his abortive efforts. That more or less closed the file on this matter.

The membership of the society at this time was 65. The minutes were becoming increasingly lengthy and it might now be questioned why it was ever considered necessary, at the request of Raymond Burn, to record the dinner menus. In March 1981 the Common Market was debated yet again. The members decided they were still in favour, but the guests took a different viewpoint.

At the Ladies Night in April the motion was that 'this house regrets the appointment of a woman prime minister'. This choice of motion seemed designed to arouse the lady guests. Margaret Thatcher had been in power for less than two years and, at this stage, it had not yet become apparent that she was to be a great premier. Bill Moyle led for the affirmative and followed a provoking line of argument by suggesting that women are temperamentally unsuited to the higher reaches of government. He cited the examples of women prime ministers so far in the world and said they had been disasters, but he didn't include Israel's Golda Meier in the list, claiming she was more like a man than a woman! He described Thatcher to be more a tin god, and a rusty one at that, than an 'iron lady'. Taking into account the events of the next few years, Moyle's arguments did not stand the test of time. Phillip Couse led for the negative. He suggested that talent not muscles were what was needed in government, and that the proposer's case was built on prejudice. When the vote was taken at the end of the meeting, the members' vote was eight all. The guests, unsurprisingly, defeated the motion by 28 votes to 13. The president, John Coward, cast his vote for the motion. It is difficult to persuade oneself that voting in favour when the member-and-guest count was so strongly against, is anything other than perverse. Some years later the president's casting vote, and how it should be exercised, was to be challenged.

It was considered at this time whether there should be some sort of differential membership subscription to maintain the financial support of inactive members, particularly as the accounts of the society were in deficit. However, this idea made no progress as it was agreed that the annual subscription was low enough already and the extra administration involved would not be justified by results.

There was a 'balloon debate' in December 1981. This involved speakers assuming certain jobs or professions and making a case for not being asked to jump out of the balloon which only had room for a single survivor. In January 1982 the subject for debate was 'that this house regrets the survival of blood sports' with George Green, a lawyer, leading for the affirmative and Donald Wasdell for the negative. The arguments put forward were familiar ones, but it was surprising that the motion was carried.

One of the casualties of the crisis in the early 1970s had been the society's involvement in the schools debating competitions which had started in 1954 for the Charles Massey Cup (for boys) and the Margaret Pugh Cup (for girls) which had been introduced five years later. The competitions appear to have lapsed and there are no records of them taking place during the remainder of the 1970s. The Literary and Debating Society of the Birmingham and Midland Institute then took up the baton in the late 1970s and, with the help of the resources and sponsorship (until 1985) of the *Birmingham Post*, brought the contest back to life. The BMI competition included girls and co-educational schools and it appears that the separate competition for the Margaret Pugh Cup was never renewed. The *Birmingham Post* gavel is still awarded to the best individual speaker in the final.

The chairman of the organising committee from 1981-85 was Andrew Peet, an occasional guest and eventual member of the Birmingham & Edgbaston Debating Society, who then worked for the *Birmingham Post & Mail*. Another key link connecting the *Birmingham Post* and the society was Brian Vertigen, a senior member of the editorial staff who became an honorary secretary and then president (1981-82). Raymond Burton, who was to be president six years later, also became involved and drew the society back into playing a part in judging the competition as it had done some fifteen years earlier. The competition since 1980 has been for the Douglas Maine Nicholls Trophy, named after a BMI lecturer who was life president of its Literary and Debating Society. The Charles Massey Cup re-appeared soon afterwards, presumably handed in by the last school to have won it, and has since been awarded to the runner-up.

Much of the credit for the growth of the competitions is owed to two teachers: husband and wife Adrian and Mary Ramsden. They joined Andrew Peet on the BMI organising committee in the mid-1980s and, as a result of their efforts, a contest that had originally involved only eight schools soon attracted an entry of over 40 from all parts of the Midlands. The Ramsdens remained involved until 2004 when Andrew Peet took up the reins again on his own. That same year he joined the society. In 1970 committee members were invited to judge the Observer Mace junior debating competition and the Birmingham Junior Chamber of Commerce competition. There is nothing in the subsequent records to suggest that this became a regular arrangement.

A motion debated in September 1982 was 'that this house believes that the Government has failed Her Majesty and her subjects both at home and abroad'. This wording sounds a little pompous to today's ears but was perhaps explained when Roger Hatton, in proposing the motion, listed insults to the Queen - the attack in The Mall and the intrusions on her privacy - at the front of a catalogue of other, arguably more serious, matters: the deaths in the Falklands, unrest in Northern Ireland and three million unemployed. Opposing, Roger Winter took a much more positive view of state of the nation. He suggested that much of what the proposer was concerned about, such as the troubles in Northern Ireland, were endemic problems that could not be blamed on one government. The motion was lost by a single vote.

Concern was expressed at the AGM in November 1982 about speeches running over time. It was agreed that the opening speeches should be of ten to twelve minutes, contributions from the floor no more than four minutes and summing up for five minutes. All this was approved. Roger Stone was concerned that some of the debates were becoming too informal and that parliamentary-style courtesies should not be neglected.

More heat was engendered when the issue of the president's casting vote was discussed. Philip Lesser suggested that it should be meaningful rather than automatic. Several former presidents had their say and views appeared to be equally divided. It was agreed that the matter should be referred to those reviewing the rules at that time. However, whilst debating a motion in December 1982 - that the house regretted the incursion of bankers into the work of other professions - the leading speaker in the negative, Christopher Tuffs, a bank manager, launched a strong tongue-in-cheek attack on the casting vote of the president, Roger Hatton, and raised doubts about the latter's impartiality because he was also a banker. Tuffs defined the church, medicine and the law as the only professions and described bankers as mere tradesmen. The motion was carried without the president's casting vote being necessary. However, the use of which the president made of his casting vote was challenged after a tied vote at the next meeting. The basis for this was not clear and it was overruled. There seems to be no good reason why the president should always cast his vote in the affirmative as if the *status quo* was thus being upheld. Tuffs, in fact, succeeded Hatton as president and, in his tribute to the latter, recalled that he had been required to make a casting vote an unprecedented three times.

A debate in 1983 on the advantages of the North-South divide led to a tie and yet more discussion about how the chairman's casting vote should be used. In this case, the chairman voted against the motion. Roger Hatton, when president, voted for the *status quo* rather than for change if the former was what a motion demanded. Former president Alan Harrison suggested that the chairman should write down in secret his vote before the house divided, but this received scant support.

In discussions with leading members of the society on the content of this book, voting and the president's casting vote were discussed at length. The key issue was whether members should vote according to their convictions on the matter under discussion, or according to which side has marshalled its arguments most effectively. In a passionate debate particularly, it is very difficult to find the detachment to vote against one's own deeply held convictions. Several of those present claimed to be disinterested enough to vote always according to the quality of the argument presented in debates. However, this is a purist approach that is almost certainly not followed by the great majority of those who participate in debates. It is hard to believe that a university society particularly would find itself able to do so.

In November 1983 the motion proposed by Roger Hatton was 'that the house believes that affairs of state must not be affected by affairs of the heart'. The choice of subject related to the publicly exposed extra-marital affair of a Conservative cabinet minister, Cecil Parkinson MP. The debate was notable for the fact that the precise meaning of the motion was claimed by some members to be open to doubt. There had been nothing in either the national or the society's debate on the matter to suggest that Parkinson's effectiveness as a senior government minister had been impaired by the affair, and the same might be said of hundreds of other politicians during the last three centuries. Whether that meant the motion should be defeated was far from clear. A motion postulating a general principle, when a particular case is in everyone's mind, does not always work as it should. In this case the debate had no clear focus and the president conceded this. However, Brian Vertigen, who led in the negative, countered by stating firmly that if one agreed with the public pronouncement of a prominent bishop on the subject (against Parkinson) one should vote against the motion. This viewpoint might not have been widely shared and the votes were tied. The motion was only carried with the president's casting vote. Under any other business, several members asked that greater care be taken in drafting motions for debate.

Having been near death a few years before, the society was rapidly regaining its strength at this time. In February 1984 there was a joint debate with the Catenian Association, an international brotherhood of Roman Catholic men, on whether beauty contests were degrading. The motion was carried by the members and the ten Catenians present by 15 votes to eleven. The four other guests made it a tie 15 - 15. The member who commented that it had been an altogether too serious argument over something that should be light-hearted fun had probably got it right. One can detect the beginnings of political correctness. One legacy of the joint debate with the Catenian Association was that Birmingham stockbroker Timothy Ryan, a future president (1997-98), joined the society.

CHAPTER 22

Margaret Thatcher stood firm in face of another miners' strike in 1984. Neil Kinnock, who succeeded Michael Foot as Labour leader, tried to modernise the party, but he could not prevent the Conservatives from winning the 1987 general election. In 1989 the iron curtain started to crumble and this was followed by German reunification in 1990. The unpopular Poll Tax was one of the reasons why Thatcher lost the support of the Conservative parliamentary party and resigned as prime minister.

A debate in December 1984 addressed the issue whether life in Britain was better in the 1930s than it was in the 1980s. The problem with this type of motion - a point made already in this narrative - is better for whom? The 1930s in Britain were a golden age for the middle-class, but virtually nobody among the members who attended the debate would have remembered first-hand what the decade was like. Unsurprisingly, the discussion degenerated into an arid exchange of statistics. Also, arguments whether labour-saving devices made life better, when the alternative was domestic servants, are bound to be sterile and inconclusive. When faced with statistics that are overwhelming, life today for the whole population is far better than it was in the 'good old days'. It might have been better to have included the words 'middle-class' in the motion. Drafted as it was, defeat was inevitable.

The President's Medallion, which is worn by presidents at meetings, was commissioned in 1984. It was designed by Dr Bernard Juby. The rationale for the design was that the top part of the medallion represents the arms of the Calthorpe family who were Lords of the Manor of Edgbaston. The gavel is self-explanatory and occupies the position of central authority. The lower part is from the *de Bermingham* coat of arms. This represents Birmingham itself and the two sides of debate over which the president presides and the black or white element in voting.

In February the society debated the economic policies of the government. The proposal was that they were wrong and a well-informed discussion followed and the society only just exonerated Mrs Thatcher's government by a single vote. The guests thought otherwise. Tony Houghton immediately challenged the count on the grounds that the vote of a member who had left early had been included. The president decided that nothing in the rules prevented this and upheld the result. The humour of the minute-taker was allowed full rein when he demonstrated his mastery of the oxymoron by recording that Houghton 'was affronted and taken aback at the same time.'

In May 1985 the motion debated was 'that this house believes that its rules should specifically exclude ladies from membership'. As a motion for debate, rather than a proposed rule change at a general meeting, the verdict of the house in itself could not change anything. Roger Winter proposed the motion, drawing the attention of the house to 140 years of tradition and the unfortunate precedent of allowing a lady (the aforementioned Sylvia Cohen) to join the society some 30 years earlier. Winter argued for the pleasures of male company and the need to speak freely in debates if necessary. He said that the society had to decide where it stood and enshrine it in a clear rule. Leading in the negative, Raymond Burton suggested that the rules quite correctly allowed the matter to be dealt with in the context of contemporary judgment. He pointed out that neither the Queen nor the Prime Minister were eligible for membership of the society. This was a questionable line of argument.

After a meeting in December 1986 the issue of female membership was raised yet again. Raymond Burn, a hard-line 'anti', reminded members about unpaid subscriptions and then referred to a member who had brought his wife as a guest to the preceding meeting. Burn considered this reprehensible and, if repeated, he would ask the committee to consider the terms under which members could bring guests. Tony Houghton criticised the use of the word 'reprehensible', particularly as the lady was not a prospective member. The president, Dr Anthony Joseph, curtailed further discussion by reminding members that there was no constitutional restriction on the attendance of lady guests and stating that he knew that not all members shared Burn's views. He directed the secretary to call an EGM on the matter if enough members wished it.

At this time the minutes were very thoroughly written, recording what all the contributors to debates had to say. An increasing strain of wry humour can also be detected. The minutes of a debate in March 1986 on the Channel Tunnel gave the secretary full rein to his humour. This continued with the next meeting when the somewhat pointless procedure of recording what was eaten allowed him to report that the meeting was 'preceded by something which appeared at first sight to be a dinner'. The avocado was described as rock hard and the prawns limp, and the report continued in the same vein. The minutes of a debate soon afterwards on politics being kept out of sport occupied five full pages in a foolscap minute book. The moderate food provided by Edgbaston Golf Club at that time led to a move to the Staff House, University of Birmingham. A good quality dinner was provided there, so no change was required in the format which was proving so successful. However, the rooms at the Staff House were divided only by sliding panels. A particularly noisy gathering in an adjacent area disrupted one of the society's debates and, as a venue, it was considered to be less than ideal.

Another discussion on whether Royalty were an expensive anachronism led to more concern about the wording of motions. Tony Houghton, opposing, claimed that the proposer, Ed Doolan, a radio personality and journalist, had defined neither 'expensive' nor 'anachronism'. He demanded that the former required the qualification 'compared to what' and said that the latter meant 'out of harmony with its time' which Royalty were not. The motion was comfortably defeated and the record reports that Houghton performed particularly well in the debate.

The society meetings returned to Edgbaston Golf Club in September 1987 after the club had promised to try harder with the catering. For this meeting members were encouraged to bring their elder or adult children and this led to 18 guests being present. The motion proposed by one of these guests, Ursula Dearman, was that the house regretted the demise of the Social Democratic Party. The SDP had been formed by four leading Labour politicians who were disillusioned with the suicidal leftward drift of their party. For the SDP to have succeeded, even after a pact with the Liberals, would have taken a lot of doing. There was a slim possibility of success in the early days but the Falklands War made Margaret Thatcher unassailable and the SDP/Liberal Alliance split the political left, allowing the Conservatives 18 years in power. During the debate no great sympathy emerged for the middle way and the motion was comfortably defeated.

In February 1988 the house persuaded itself by a wide margin, or was persuaded by Tony Houghton, to support the Community Charge. Taking into account what was to follow, the society's collective judgment on this issue was questionable. Attendance levels and the slow paying of annual subscriptions were a concern throughout the 1980s. Raymond Burton was re-elected as president for an extra year in October 1988 because his efforts to increase membership were working but needed more time to be completed. The meeting ended with Geoffrey Crofts raising the issue of women members yet again. After some more argument on the matter, the president promised that it would be considered further.

At this time Tony Grazier was debates secretary and a number of innovations were introduced to 'freshen up' the society. For a trial period guests were invited at half-price, name badges were introduced and the year's programme of motions was published in the handbook. There was also a younger persons' evening in each session. That some of these innovations should have fallen into disuse, rather than there being a positive decision to discontinue them, is a not unfamiliar situation in the administration of small bodies.

In January 1989 the society debated whether enlightened censorship is needed to protect the public. It never ceases to surprise that business and professional people cling to some form of censorship without considering whose taste or judgment is to be the norm. Reassuringly, the motion was defeated. At the annual ladies' evening in May 1989 the debate was attended by 12 members and 35 guests, an unsatisfactory imbalance. The motion was that blood sports should be abolished and two guest speakers led for the affirmative and negative: James Barrington, executive director of the League Against Cruel Sports, and Ian Coghill, publicity officer of the British Field Sports Society. Both speakers performed brilliantly and the members present divided seven votes to five against the motion but, with guests taking into account, the vote was 27 - 20 in favour. The sparse membership attendance must have been a disappointment to Tony Grazier who organised this debate. Guest speakers, on occasion, prevent the society from an introverted drift towards declining standards of debate unmeasured against anything from outside. However, guests speakers were invited again on a more recent occasion to debate GM crops and some recall that what ensued was a little 'over their heads'.

At the AGM in October 1989 it was reported that membership had fallen from 60 (two years ago) to 45. The president stressed the importance of guests who would add to the quality of the debate and be potential members. He also referred to the frequent discussions about women members and explained that a clear consensus on this issue had not emerged, so therefore things should be left as they are. This ruling was never going to please everyone and a referendum on the matter was suggested.

Secretary Derek Beanland's beautifully written minutes - both in handwriting and content - were applauded. It was suggested by Geoffrey Crofts that he made reality sound more exciting than it actually was. Crofts hoped that this would continue, particularly as he was leading for the affirmative that same evening on the subject of belief in life after death. The motion was carried following a somewhat inconclusive debate.

At a ladies' night in 1990 the motion was that feminism had caused a decline in love and romance. Mrs Jackie Houghton led for the affirmative. She drew attention to the changes in women's lives that had ended romantic love in the Jane Austen mould - something which she added had, in any case, been a middle-class phenomenon. The working classes were, she said, rougher and less sentimental. Opposing, Mrs Angela Taylor said that men saw feminism as threatening but, in spite of that, romantic fiction, flowers and St Valentine's Day cards were all enjoying boom sales. Contributions from the floor were amusing and the motion was comfortably defeated. In the same 1990-91 session the house also debated the death penalty for premeditated murder and defeated it, as it did the re-introduction of national service a month later. As both these could be described as right wing positions, the society showed a welcome moderation.

Tony Grazier, who was to be president from 1994 to 1996 and was progressive on the issue of female membership, had, when debates secretary, done what he could to involve ladies and on one occasion organised two husband and wife teams: Alan Harrison (president 1979-80) and Raymond Burton (1987-89) and their spouses. The dearth of female members was because so few ladies applied for membership after 1956 and, had more done so, the matter would probably have resolved itself much earlier. Grazier organised the debate to soften opposition to female membership. He recognised that going round an obstacle that cannot be removed might have some tactical merit. The fact was that opponents of female membership, at this time, usually managed to deflect discussion of the matter whenever it was raised. Raymond Burn, the president in 1990, was an entrenched opponent of ladies being members, but he wrote an appreciative report of the Houghton/Taylor debate including the words 'our ladies night broke with all the traditions of the society...their wit, charm and repartee provided members with a truly enjoyable and entertaining evening'.

The new session began in September when the finalists in the schools competition were invited to lead in the affirmative and negative. The motion was about the United Nations, to which the society gave its support. This meeting was held at the Birmingham Club in Ethel Street. It was felt that a new venue in the centre of Birmingham might reverse falling attendances. This, of course, depended on where members worked and whether it suited them to go straight from the office to a debate. The club, whilst well appointed, could not provide a suitable ambiance for a debate, and having to disband into the centre of Birmingham at 11pm would not have appealed to ladies particularly. In April 1991 ladies' night was taken back to Edgbaston Golf Club, and the experiment with the Birmingham Club as a venue was short-lived.

At the 1990 AGM concern was expressed about falling membership. Amongst the ideas discussed were advertising for members, outside speakers and topic-led debates. Spencer Comley died in 1990, and this meant that Kenneth Wilkinson was assumed to be his successor as the oldest living member and thus 'father of the house'. Wilkinson had joined the society in 1950 and been its president twice. At a later meeting it was reported that another possible claimant, Peter Osler (president 1947-48), had joined the society in 1928 and was still alive, but whether he was an active member appeared to be open to doubt and he must have been a very old man by this time.

At the next AGM there was a proposal to amend the rules that referred to the time allocation for speeches, which were being ignored. A seemingly innocent suggestion that the wording of the two rules should also be amended at the same time to include the feminine triggered off yet another discussion on the desirability of lady members.

Speaking to a motion that the 1980s had been a decade to be regretted, Tony Houghton catalogued the failures of the Thatcher government and Richard Cliff its successes. The latter amusingly suggested that the house should not allow the present recession to colour its judgment - a recession so bad that even the firms who had no intention of paying had stopped ordering! The motion was only just defeated but, with guests included, it was carried. Two years after the decade ended, it seems that the earlier glories of the Thatcher years had been forgotten.

The voting after society debates usually follows a pattern that involves a count of the votes of the members first, and then of the votes of the members and visitors combined. This is not the normal procedure in a joint debate when the votes of the entire house are counted. That had also been the case in the public debates held in the nineteenth century, particularly when the non-members outnumbered the members by a wide margin. The reader might wonder why people who have participated fully in every other aspect of the debate should be effectively disenfranchised when it comes to the vote, especially if they account for two-thirds or more of those present. If the two counts are at variance, there is a lack of clarity about which side has truly won. The explanation of this, as so often, lies with tradition, but it could be an isolated example of the society taking itself too seriously.

By this time part of the secretary's responsibility had been hived off in order to share out the work: a dinner secretary and a debates secretary were appointed. This division of responsibilities has proved effective. The debates secretary chooses the motions and invites the leading speakers. Members are not expected to refuse the call without very good reason. It was recalled by a member of the committee that the debates secretary was to be known as the 'motions secretary'. The member in line for the job would not take it until the name had been changed! The dinner secretary deals with the venue and the catering. The main secretarial role involves taking the minutes, looking after constitutional matters, calling meetings and generally fulfilling the normal duties of a secretary of a committee-run organisation. The structure had started to take shape since Roger Stone took responsibility for running the first dinner debates in 1973. Ideally, the incumbents are expected to serve at least three years in these offices

In October 1990 Roger Hatton led for the negative against a motion proposed by Tony Grazier that the house would refuse to sacrifice its sons for Kuwait. Prior to the debate, Hatton handed out some paperwork and used visual aids during his speech. Eyebrows were raised at this 'sales conference' procedure and John Taylor made a good-humoured protest. The latter is well known for the effectiveness of his impromptu interventions in debate.

CHAPTER 23

John Major won a narrow and somewhat surprising victory in the 1992 general election. The Labour leader, Neil Kinnock, resigned the leadership and was replaced by John Smith. The latter died three years later and opened the way for Tony Blair to lead Labour to three successive victories.

The minutes of meetings in the early 1990s covered debates in great detail, perhaps to an excessive extent. They almost became too long to be read at meetings regardless of the wit with which they were written. In 1994 some minutes of meetings were typed, but generally that was exceptional. The handwriting of secretaries during the life of the society varied from the exquisite to the indecipherable.

Since the early 1990s the motions were generally better chosen and there were fewer than usual on abstract issues. On ladies night in April 1994 the house debated political correctness for the first time. The motion stated that it was the curse of the age and those speaking in the negative attempted to argue that, whilst it was tiresome, there were more serious problems that deserved to be considered the curse of the age. This line of argument was enough to tie the votes of members and guests 25 - 25. The members alone carried the motion by twelve votes to seven. One of the speakers in this debate was Terry Arthur, a member of the society who had been an England Rugby Football international some thirty years earlier.

The motion chosen for ladies night in March 1995 was one which had been debated in 1931: that professionalism was ruining sport. Some of the speakers appeared to suggest that professionalism affected the way games are played - too much emphasis on defence and safety. Perhaps the most sensible contribution came from a guest, a Mrs Fulham, who asked if the choice of this motion for ladies night was designed to keep them away! Some members argued that professionalism was synonymous with bad sportsmanship and corruption, and this interpretation drew a protest from Jim Fergus, a future president of the society. The motion was carried.

By 1993 the society had begun to consider its coming sesquicentennial (due in 1996). As might have been expected of a debating society, there was some sparring over whether the word *sesqui-centenary* actually existed and if it should be hyphenated (the answers are almost certainly no on both counts). This was, no doubt, amusing but hardly stimulated meaningful progress. For some unexplained reason the committee had a problem in finding out the actual date of the first meeting in 1846 and went as far as setting up a sub-committee under Philip Lesser, a former president (1991-92) to investigate. However, in October 1994 Tony Grazier, an effective organiser, was due to become president. It was obvious to him and others that his term of office would have to span two years in order to embrace the responsibility for - and the organising of - the sesquicentennial from beginning to end. This arrangement was agreed by the committee in June 1994. At the same meeting Tony Houghton was given the task of researching for and producing a handbook history of the society and was appointed to serve as vice-president, also for a two-year period or 'for a shorter term if reviewed as necessary'.

The customary arrangement was that the vice-president was president elect, but Houghton had already been president for two years (1973-75). Today, those present at that committee meeting twelve years ago had difficulty in recalling the rationale behind this appointment and it was misconstrued inevitably by some members of the society at the time who assumed Houghton to be in line for another term as president. Grazier's appointment as president for two years meant that there was certainly a vacancy for a vice-president in the first of those two years until his ultimate successor was chosen. The minutes on the matter are ambiguous and it is possible that Houghton himself misunderstood the situation. An explanation, presumably confirmed at the AGM in October, that Houghton's appointment was in recognition of his role in the sesquicentennial planning and that he was not in line to inherit the presidency appears to have satisfied everyone.

There were further discussions about the planned sesquicentennial celebrations at all the committee meetings during the year and also at the next AGM in October 1995 when it was reported that one event would be a special dinner and debate to be held on ladies' night. Recalling Mrs Fulham's comments at the earlier debate in March, it was suggested by Roger Hatton that a motion of interest to ladies be chosen. Grazier countered by saying that what appeared to be a poor choice of motion could still lead to a good debate. At the same meeting there was an inconclusive discussion about the handbook history which, it was admitted, was falling behind schedule. Neither members of the committee nor Houghton himself had much knowledge of the society's history and this could only have been rectified by frequent visits to the Birmingham Central Library where the records were stored. Although some progress had been made, the handbook history was never completed.

Houghton was a witty debater, possibly one of the best so far in the life of the society, and his fellow members, many of them still involved today, remember him as a performer rather than as an organiser. Because of this, Grazier asked the secretary Michael Holt, an architect, a talented amateur artist and an expert on ancient Greece (on which he lectured on cruise ships), to play a bigger role in the organisation of the celebrations. Holt died in his late sixties in 1998 when he was vice-president of the society and in line to succeed Timothy Ryan as president.

As part of the celebrations, there was a combined debate in November with the University of Birmingham. The debate on a united Europe was tied twelve against twelve (members and the university) and the president gave his casting vote in favour. With guests also included, the vote was 19 to 18 in favour. This debate helped to establish the regular annual meeting with the Birmingham University Debating Society. It also brought up the question of how votes were taken after debates. The usual pattern had been to count the members' vote as if it was the only one that mattered, and the second count, which included guests, was for interest only. A 'joint debate' suggests equal status between the two societies taking part and, in the opinion of the president, courtesy required that there should be one unified count of the votes. This vote did not include, of course, the guests unconnected with either society. Raymond Burn made a traditionalist protest against the proposed change, but he had little support. The rules now distinguish between routine guests and members of another society involved in a joint debate. Around this time the regular joint debates with the Oxford and Cambridge Unions ceased. The demands on the time of their presidents made it increasingly difficult to find suitable dates.

The sesquicentennial dinner took place at Edgbaston Golf Club on 1st May 1996 attended by 120 members, their ladies and some honoured guests. The Lord Mayor was represented by Alderman Peter Barwell, and Professor R. J. Scott attended on behalf of the University of Birmingham. Interestingly, whether the Lord Mayor was to be invited had been left in abeyance for a while after a member pointed out that the society pre-dated the corporation by a wide margin of years. The president, Tony Grazier, spoke about the history of the society and Professor Scott proposed its health. The latter's speech was recalled as 'witty and brilliant' in the minutes. The reply was from Kenneth Wilkinson, who had been the 'father of the house' for some years by then and still is so at the time of writing. The debate that the quality of life is better now than it was 150 years ago inevitably started late as a result. Tony Houghton proposed and Professor Redvers Garside opposed. Both made good speeches, Houghton particularly when one considers that he had left his notes at home and wasn't prepared to go back for them! However, the time taken by the dinner and then Garside meant that summings-up had to be dispensed with. It is difficult to believe that a motion like this could be defeated, but defeated it was by the members 19 votes to nine and, with guests counted, by 54 votes to 37.

When the 1996-97 session began a new secretary, Conrad Charles, laid out the minutes in what might be described as more business-like format which made them easier to read than previous secretaries' continuous prose with no paragraph breaks. At the AGM in October, with the sesquicentennial celebrations completed, Tony Grazier yielded the presidency with much acclaim and he was succeeded by Richard Cliff, a Birmingham solicitor.

In February 1997, when the Conservative government led by John Major was about to lose power, the society debated that New Labour is 'champagne socialism' writ large. Interestingly, an earlier assumption of the author that the Labour party would never have mustered enough backing within the society to reflect its support in the country was called into question by the result in this debate. The vote of the members was tied ten against ten and the chairman cast his vote in favour.

At the AGM in October 1997 there were discussions about whether ladies should be admitted as members. Conrad Charles claimed that the matter had been settled in 1956 and the election of Sylvia Cohen in December of that year would appear to have been proof enough. However, the faulty procedure in 1956 has already been referred to, and with no women elected since the early 1960s and Roger Stone's amendment in 1977, things appeared to be back where they were pre-1956. But were they? The issue now was no longer about interpreting the intentions of the founding fathers of the society, but the actual wording of the rule as currently amended. The entire matter had not been handled over the years with any certitude and why nobody referred to the past minute books is difficult to understand, unless it was the inconvenience of visiting the Central Library. Tony Grazier suggested a society referendum, a sensible enough course of action which would have involved all members in the decision, not just those present at a meeting. Geoffrey Crofts argued that blackballing could cause embarrassment for female candidates, but the truth is that blackballing in any circumstances causes embarrassment for membership candidates, and for their proposers and seconders. What Crofts and others appeared to be arguing for was qualified blackballing with objections on the ground of gender rendered invalid. But blackballing with reasons having to be given is not blackballing in any true sense. If the procedure is intended to keep out the obnoxious, one should remember that women can be obnoxious too. Unsurprisingly, there were pleas from others that the society should not be driven by a desire to be politically correct.

The matter of ladies came up again almost inevitably at the 1998 AGM. Tony Grazier suggested that reasons should be given for blackballs, thus allowing the committee to decide whether a blackball is justified. The discussion that followed was long and convoluted, with the points made by each member being dictated by where he stood on the issue rather than the procedure. The policy of excluding women had already been undermined by the membership of Sylvia Cohen and four others 40 years earlier, and by the admission of lady guests to debates over many years and a perennial shortage of members. It would be easier to understand the exclusion of women from a rugby football or cricket club - games that few of them play - than from a debating society. The meeting decided that the committee should be convened with only this issue on its agenda in order to submit a recommendation to the next AGM.

At the AGM in October 1999 the matter of ladies was to be raised yet again based on the belief that there was nothing in the constitution that specifically prohibited them from membership. Because of the vote in 1977, this line of argument was no longer as fallacious as it had been until 1956. Others re-stated their belief that the voting procedure remained an obstacle to the admission of women. In the end it was decided to leave the entire matter in abeyance for the time being. Soon afterwards the committee voted against calling an EGM on the issue of female membership. This was too much for Conrad Charles, a supporter of female membership, and he resigned from the committee and the society.

An unusual motion in December 1997 was that the house believed that, if God applied for the job again, he would not be short-listed. Most of the speakers treated the motion lightly and this led to some entertaining speeches. Tony Houghton led for the affirmative and claimed that God had done little since the Earth began 4½ million years ago. It appears that nobody corrected him that Earth had, in fact, begun 4½ billion years ago. The minute-taker did not pick up on the error which was repeated three times in the record. Leading for the negative, Dr Joseph, always an entertaining speaker, told members that they could not expect a rabbinic contribution from him and then claimed that Earth began only 5,758 years ago, a somewhat suspect calculation. There are, of course, still a few whose literal belief in the Bible allows them to calculate, from a certain amount of begetting recorded in the Book of Genesis, that the creation happened in a single week in 4004 BC. The motion was defeated.

The president Timothy Ryan introduced a bell in February 1998 to curtail speeches that ran over time. He was challenged good-humouredly on the grounds that this was a unilateral action. In the badinage that followed, the president came out on top. Ryan had a propensity for quoting historical facts to sustain debating points. His successor, Tony Ridgway, sought rule changes that would help clear the path to female membership. Philip Gretton, who followed him as president, was less sympathetic to that cause but the changes initiated by Ridgway when he was president were adopted eventually. One of these changes, the subject of an EGM in October 2000, was the repeal of the rule that no candidate shall be elected if three votes by members present were unfavourable. Rejected candidates could not re-apply for twelve months. The change agreed was that the votes of one third of those members present was required to reject a candidate. One might wonder why anybody would want to be a member of a club or society if one third or more of the members had voted for rejection, until it is realised that the purpose behind the change to the rules was to prevent a determined minority from blackballing female candidates for membership. The revised rule was approved by 14 votes to six.

By now it was obvious that those against women members were fighting a losing battle and their resistance effectively ended with this rule change. The way the matter had been dealt with throughout had been unsatisfactory and at no time was the issue ever put to the membership asking for a straight yes or no answer. Instead there had been, for almost fifty years, a nibbling away at the edges with amendments to the wording of rules, some of them drafted in 1846. In doing this, it would have been understandable if some members had not realised the full significance of any proposed changes. Effectively, the 'losing battle' had been a rearguard action ever since Sylvia Cohen was admitted as a member in 1956. Her election did not 'open the floodgates' and only four ladies followed her in the next few years. Since 2000 the ladies joining the society have been wives or daughters of members and there are very few who could be described as 'independent'. The expected flood has not so far materialised. With the issue of female membership finally settled, Conrad Charles was invited to rejoin the society three months later.

There was an attempt at an EGM in 2004 to amend the rules by introducing the wording 'that the society was open to all, irrespective of their age (subject to a minimum age of 18 years), race or nationality, religion or lack of religious belief, sex or sexual orientation, socio-economic background or political inclination'. An amendment in the name of Professor Hilbourne proposed that the word 'disability' be added and that was agreed. The amended resolution clearly did not appeal to the members who believed that it pandered to political correctness and, when no proposer could be found, it fell. One might add quite rightly too! Professor Hilbourne, a partially sighted man now always accompanied by his guide dog, is another of the society's characters and a very fine speaker in debate.

Reflecting on the long running saga of female membership, or on the emancipation of women generally, men are bound to ask themselves if it was just prejudice after all. The argument had generated some heat at times, but it did not divide the society irreparably. In some cases, presidents were frustrated by their committees and found themselves and their successors in opposite camps. There were others who objected on principle to the attempts to achieve the desired result by constitutional tinkering, even though they were sympathetic to the cause. It was almost bound to be a losing struggle as every vote against women members was a battle won, but the war would have gone on. One vote in favour would have been enough to end the matter irreversibly. When the society was founded there were no career women and their role in life was entirely domestic. Membership of any sort of club or society was simply not an issue. But things began to change, slowly at first, in the 1860s. The battle for emancipation had been more or less won by 1918. That did not mean that men-only clubs ceased to exist, but a number of doors had opened to women. In some ways not a lot changed in social attitudes between 1918 and 1960: this was Noël Coward's England in time of peace and war, and Sapper's Bulldog Drummond and Ian Fleming's James Bond would have found each other congenial companions. But the 1960s brought many changes, including a more militant feminism which set into motion the feminisation of society. Then came Margaret Thatcher's premiership, but she could hardly be described as an icon of feminism and she soon became an 'ism' herself. She proved that a woman leader could be tough with foreigners and not be afraid to declare war, thus winning the respect of men. The next phase in the battle of the sexes was political correctness, which is with us still. It is an irritant that tends to reinforce prejudice against women and minority groups who believe that there is still some way to go, or another hurdle to be overcome, while others who consider themselves to be fair-minded think that liberalisation has gone far enough. But that, of course, is a microcosm of the political battle through the ages. A debating society, which models itself on the House of Commons, was perhaps not the best place for a last ditch stand against the encroachment of women. Debating, like politics, is generally regarded as a unisex activity and the matter would probably have been settled earlier if it were not for the dinners at which some men will always prefer male company. The society has not subsequently been overrun by women wanting to join and those that have will be considered by many to have refreshed the society. The need to recruit new members is one that will never go away and now, in the twenty-first century, it will be seen that virtue has been made of necessity.

CHAPTER 24

The new Millennium was celebrated worldwide and rather expensively in Great Britain with the dome built in Greenwich. Tony Blair began to lose popularity after aligning the government with the USA in the Iraq War of 2003. The war had gone better than the post-war reconstruction. After the defeat of the Conservatives in the 2005 general election the party leader Michael Howard resigned and was succeeded by a much younger David Cameron.

Kenneth Wilkinson, the father of the house, completed 50 years in membership in 2000 and he was presented with a tankard. He joined the society in October 1950. In March 2001 the society debated a motion that the Tories did not deserve to be returned to power. Only four years after they had lost power in 1997, it was, the house decided, too early for a return, in spite of its Conservative sympathies. In December of the same year the motion was whether there was no greater nuisance than mobile phones. The points raised in discussion replicated the arguments that were used in past debates against cars, aeroplanes and almost any modern invention. Reassuringly, the motion was defeated. The society debated in January 2002 whether the lifestyle of Prince Charles was a more relevant public example than that of his mother. This was the sort of motion that would have been unthinkable in the more respectful 1950s and earlier. Amongst members the vote was tied. Before the president was able to cast his vote in favour, there was a discussion on whether Roger Stone had been entitled to vote on the grounds that he had arrived late and not heard all the arguments. Tony Grazier, accepted at the time as the foremost authority in the society on rules, was consulted and Stone's vote stood.

After the debate the president, Richard Tudor, asked whether minutes should be read at meetings when they could just as easily be circulated. This suggestion, he said, had come from the guests. The fact was that the minutes had being getting very lengthy, almost to the point of recording what everybody said in debates *verbatim*, rather than being a summary of the arguments put forward. The minutes were also cluttered needlessly by dinner menus. It was apparent that the procedure of reading the minutes of five or six pages was taking too much time, but the response from the traditionalist members was somewhat mixed and the matter was referred back to the president for further consideration and he decided that the minutes should continue to be read. Tudor, an orthopaedic surgeon, was asked to serve a second term as president. This, as it happened, also suited his putative successor, Geoffrey Oakley, who was also to be a positive president (2003-04). Tudor enjoyed riding to hounds and he was a son-in-law of the former society president David Lowe (1951-52), as also was Ian Marshall (president 2004-05). The latter is a partner in the legal firm, Martineau Johnson (formerly Ryland, Martineau & Co), the history of which is interwoven with that of the society itself. Tudor had assiduously pursued the issues of more members, increased attendances and improved standards of debate. The one-year presidential term, however, remains the norm for the society and it would be invidious if a second year were to be some sort of accolade offered to some and withheld from others. It is possible, however, to argue that the one-year term, effectively only eight months from October to May, is too short to introduce radical changes. Is the role of the president merely to preside over the society as he finds it, or to act as some sort of catalyst for innovation and reform? The single-year term of office allows more members to be president and that strengthens the society administratively: nearly all the presidents of the society appear to have served it well and the best time for innovation, as any politician knows, is in the early days of a new administration. A critic, however, might suggest that a stasis has permeated the society since the dinner debates were introduced over 30 years ago and, sooner or later, policies to attract younger members have to be put in place.

After the next debate Geoffrey Crofts raised again the matter of reading the minutes. Another member suggested that minutes from the far distant past would be more interesting, but it was pointed out by Tony Grazier that these were nearly always very brief. The society, in fact, had gone from one extreme to the other. The longer minutes of this period of time will convey to those who follow hereafter some typical attitudes on the politics of the day. Sadly, the society's Victorian predecessors have denied today's members any knowledge of their political viewpoints, except from what is deducible from the voting.

The society debated at its next meeting whether positive discrimination is inferior to equal opportunities. There were seven lady guests present, three of them from the Birmingham University Debating Society, and the motion had been clearly chosen as 'appropriate'. The BUDS president Megan Shute, leading against the motion, put forward a powerful case for positive discrimination but the motion was still carried.

In December 2002 the monarchy was again debated: the motion being that the house would not mourn its passing. The debate was massively one-sided and the motion was defeated by 19 votes to four. Five of the six guests also voted against and one abstained. As far as the society was concerned, the monarchy had its support. In February 2003 the society returned to a repeated theme: that censorship was necessary to protect the young. This time the vote was tied 11 – 11 and the president's casting vote was against the motion. Some members challenged this on the grounds of precedent. The argument that the chairman of the meeting must, without being able to exercise any discretion, vote in favour of a motion just because the opposition has not made its case, would render the casting vote meaningless. The society debated a motion in December 2004 that the input of the Royal Family was welcomed in matters of public debate. Geoffrey Oakley, who often played a prominent part in debates concerning royalty, led for the negative. The motion was carried.

In March 2005 Camilla Gilmore was elected a member at the age of 19 years and three months. She is the daughter of Stephen Gilmore who succeeded Jim Fergus as president in October 2006. The meeting had its attention drawn to the fact that she was the youngest member ever. However, this was not true as we know of Robert Francis Martineau who was a founder member of the Edgbaston society at the age of 15, and his older brother Thomas was only 18. Joseph Chamberlain no less joined the Edgbaston Debating Society in society in 1854 when he was 18 years old. Although the merger with Birmingham's society did not happen until a year later, the Birmingham & Edgbaston Debating Society was built mainly on the provenance of the Edgbaston Debating Society. Many of the founding members of the Edgbaston society were very young at the time. The second Birmingham society had a rule that members had to be at least 18 years old and the need for it suggests that some youngsters must have been knocking at the door. It was probably introduced because the rival Edgbaston society had members of that age or even younger and, as has been observed already, the average age of Birmingham's membership was higher. However, what is certain is that Camilla Gilmore was the youngest person to join the society for a very long time.

An innovation in 2002 was the Houghton Cup, in memory of the popular Tony Houghton, which was to be awarded annually for significant contributions over time to the activities of the society. The first recipient was Bill Caswell, a former honorary secretary, to whom it was presented by Houghton's eldest daughter Angela Cloke. It then went to debates secretary

Chris Baker in 2003, Tony Grazier in 2004, a bank manager of the old school who played such an important part in the sesquicentennial celebrations, and Geoffrey Burcher who, as honorary secretary, was involved in the organisation of the schools debating competitions, in 2005. Burcher handed over his responsibilities as secretary to Roger Stone in 2004, but became honorary treasurer in October 2006, succeeding Christopher Warren. Tony Grazier had to be presented with the cup (which is, in fact, a tankard) on two separate occasions as the then secretary, Roger Stone, had mislaid the it and the first presentation was consequently of a replica. In May 2006 the cup was awarded to another former secretary Conrad Charles for his research work, particularly for that required for this book.

At a meeting in April 2005 Dr Joseph proposed a motion that voting is a waste of time and took the unusual step of asking his supporters not to vote at the end of the debate. Only one vote was cast in favour and the number of abstentions recorded suggests that the motion might otherwise have been carried. Joseph is one of the many luminaries that make the society what it is today. Other loyal supporters of the society today who have not been mentioned previously – or mentioned only fleetingly - in this narrative include Sir Robert Dowling, who was knighted for his work as headmaster of the George Dixon comprehensive which had been in decline since its great days as the George Dixon Grammar School; Roger Pritchett, who can be guaranteed to express what the right of the political spectrum is thinking; Chris Baker, who is debates secretary and now vice-president; David Barker, the dinner secretary; Geoffrey Crofts, David Slade, Ted Behague, Reg Willsher and Tim Ryan, all past presidents; John Taylor, a former secretary who also did a long stint as schools debating competition liaison officer; and Charles Barwell who represents the younger generation on the committee.

When Stephen Gilmore took over the presidency in October 2006 he experimented at the first debate over which he presided with a procedure recently adopted by the Birmingham University Debating Society. This is to take a vote before a debate starts. This allows it to be seen if there has been a movement of opinion during the debate. Unlike the university society the vote was not taken to be part of the process of judging which side 'wins' a debate with the result depending on the movement of opinion, rather than the traditional count. The Birmingham & Edgbaston society has, so far, always settled the issue by the votes of members. This debate in this case was on the merits of the Prime Minister, Tony Blair, when compared to those of his putative successor, Gordon Brown. As it happened the votes at the start were 16 to five in favour of Blair with a few abstentions. Geoffrey Oakley, opposing, faced an uphill task but he won a number of members round to his point of view and the final count was 11 - 11. The guests also supported him. Gilmore also gave his casting vote to the Brown supporters.

After the conclusion of another debate in 2006, Roger Stone referred again to the point that he and Kenneth Wilkinson had raised on several occasions in the past: that members and guests should preface their remarks 'Mr President Sir'. Whilst no doubt he was correct in this, the president did not make it mandatory, probably because he considered it would have led to repetitious points of order. Nonetheless, little is lost by reminding members of correct procedure and calling upon the society to respect its traditions. In its 160 years of history so far, it has always done so.

EPILOGUE

When the Edgbaston and the first Birmingham societies were formed in 1846 the primary motivation of the founders was to educate themselves as speakers. This was in itself an accomplishment, but some of them, whether or not they foresaw it at the time, were eventually to put it to good use by making a mark in the municipal politics of Birmingham. Set-piece debates offered young men the opportunity to hone their speaking skills and, in the early days of the society, it was men in their early twenties who predominated.

In the Victorian high noon physical pursuits emerged as an alternative to intellectual activity, but they were no great threat to the debating society which began to prosper. The leading politicians then - Peel, Palmerston, Gladstone and Disraeli - seemed like giants and their words and deeds were followed avidly in the newspapers by the educated sector of the populace which had no sporting heroes or film stars to worship. The society met to debate what the giants themselves had debated and its members felt that, in some small way, their arguments and votes contributed to the movement of opinion.

Looking back, the political life of the nation seems to have been a lot more exciting than it is today. Imperialism, Home Rule, the Parliament Act, the fall of Asquith and the Coalition Government in the Great War, the Treaty of Versailles and its consequences, the fall of Neville Chamberlain, the rise of the Labour Party and Attlee's first ministry. There was plenty to debate. Today's arid political landscape and the polarisation of opinion seem less stimulating.

On several occasions the committee has exhorted members to support the society better. Often these appeals coincided with periods when support, with hindsight, can be seen to have been at high levels. Nonetheless, committees have a duty to concern themselves with such matters and to spot clouds on the horizon.

The period between the wars is seen now as some sort of interlude. At the time, they were golden years for some and not for others. Were they wasted years? Possibly. Could the disaster of the second war have been avoided? Possibly also. But the nation's and the world's minds had switched off, leaving the stage to political opportunists.

In the years immediately after the 1939-45 war there was a desire to live life again to the full, and to socialise with one's peers. This too helped the society to thrive. But the cloud on this horizon was the spread of television broadcasting and, to the tired man of business, an evening at home began to appeal as much as an evening out. One must also add that there were other forms of entertainment and the increasing opportunity to participate in sport as well as watching it.

Downward spirals are difficult to stop: dull and sparsely attended debates only persuade the few who do take part to question whether it was worth the effort. In its moment of crisis in 1970, the society was saved by a few good men who introduced the dinner debate. Whilst the society has since continued to thrive, there are still clouds of a different sort on the horizon. The society needs to remind itself how young were its founder members. Older members fade away and their passions go with them as they become more cynical and world-weary. However, past generations have been more clubbable than today's young, but the latter will attach less importance to that aspect of the society's life and more to the debate itself. They will want to consider issues which arouse strongly held opinions rather than merely insouciant wit. The confrontational aspect of debate adds to the excitement and it should not be lost. Perhaps the seating arrangements of the Commons, or the Oxford and Cambridge Unions, could be adopted to achieve this.

The society attracted many young men who were later to develop a commitment to civic duty. Some made their marks in municipal politics first and then became Members of Parliament. In 1846 their ambitions would not have been aimed this high: Birmingham had no parliamentary representation until the Great Reform Bill of 1832 which allocated it two members. In spite of this, society members who became MPs were Joseph Chamberlain, Jesse Collings, George Dixon, William Kenrick, Sir John Benjamin Stone, Neville Chamberlain, Sir Francis Lowe, Walter Higgs, Sir Patrick Hannon, Gordon Matthews, Sir Peter Bennett, James Bowker, Leonard Cleaver, Sir Reginald Eyre and Sir Anthony Beaumont Dark. Five of them were Privy Councillors and one was a Prime Minister. This was an exceptional achievement by any standards and it is difficult to predict whether anything like it can be replicated in what will be the very different circumstances of the next 100 years.

As this history closes, the society is attracting increasingly large attendances and those who come want to speak in the debates. Whatever their motives, they are learning from it and enjoying it. The society is now held 'in trust' for future generations by those who run it and participate in it. It must never be allowed to die.

Presidents of the Edgbaston Debating Society

1846-47	Francis Owen Clark
1847-48	Thomas Martineau
1848-49	Herbert Wright
1849-50	Algernon Clark/Edward Taylor
1850-51	William Ridout Wills
1851-52	Thomas Martineau
1852-53	Samuel Timmins
1853-54	William Mathews
1854-55	W Thomas Watts

Presidents of the second Birmingham Debating Society

1850-51	James Timmins Chance
1851-52	James Timmins Chance
1852-53	George Jabet
1853-54	Dr J P Heslop
1854-55	George Dixon

Presidents of the Birmingham & Edgbaston Debating Society

1855-56	Henry Chance
1856-57	Clement Mansfield Ingleby LL D
1857-58	Cornelius T Saunders
1858-59	John Thackray Bunce
1859-60	George James Johnson
1860-61	Charles E Mathews
1861-62	John Henry Chamberlain
1862-63	Joseph Chamberlain
1863-64	Sebastian Evans MA
1864-65	William Harris
1865-66	George Spencer Mathews MA
1866-67	William Kenrick MA
1867-68	John P Turner
1868-69	Robert Francis Martineau

1869-70	Alfred Caddick
1870-71	John Alfred Langford LL D
1871-72	John Alfred Langford LL D
1872-73	Howard S Smith
1873-74	Thomas C Lowe BA
1874-75	Archibald E Park
1875-76	W H Ryland
1876-77	H Lakin Smith BA
1877-78	Charles A Harrison
1878-79	Arthur J Phillp
1879-80	Francis Lowe
1880-81	Edward Malins MD
1881-82	T Grosvenor Lee BA
1882-83	Rev E F M McCarthy MA
1883-84	J Sampson Gamgee FRSE
1884-85	Alfred C Osler
1885-86	Edward M Madden MB
1886-87	W Fowler Carter BA
1887-88	Dr Alfred H Carter
1888-89	Edward Henry Lee BA
1889-90	Dr Showell Rogers MA, LL D
1890-91	Henry Eales
1891-92	Jordan Lloyd FRCS, MD
1892-93	Cecil Crosskey
1893-94	Rev Thomas G Clarke MA
1894-95	E Bickerton Williams
1895-96	Rt Hon Joseph Chamberlain MP, LL D, DCL
1896-97	Thomas W Ryland BA
1897-98	Charles E Martineau MA
1898-99	S D Balden
1899-1900	Phineas H Levi
1900-01	Arthur D Brooks
1901-02	Dr James W Russell MA
1902-03	S M Slater MA, BCL
1903-04	R H Herbert Creak
1904-05	Gardner Tyndall
1905-06	Siward James
1906-07	Bertram G Grimley BA, LL B
1907-08	Bertram O Pemberton

1908-09	Albert Lucas FRCS
1909-10	Neville Chamberlain JP
1910-11	A R Rann
1911-12	Arthur D Mathews JP
1912-13	Frank Roscoe
1913-14	Fitz-James Sawyer MA
1914-15	J Lawrence Hawkes
1915-16	William C Camm
1916-17	Richard A Willes
1917-18	Gerald Botteley
1918-19	Thomas B Hooper
1919-20	L Arthur Smith
1920-21	Rev George W Clarke BA
1921-22	Harry Jackson
1922-23	G Austin Baker
1923-24	C Napier-Claverling
1924-25	Julian C Osler
1925-26	Bernard Parker
1926-27	Thomas H Varcoe
1927-28	Norman Wall
1928-29	Walter L Chance
1929-30	Thomas L Kennedy
1930-31	Wilfred C Matthews
1931-32	R Wynne Frazier
1932-33	W J Guest
1933-34	Laurence Cox
1934-35	Kenneth Wood
1935-36	Hubert W Neep
1936-37	F J Murray
1937-38	John F Bourke
1938-39	Herbert W Wilkes
1939-40	Herbert W Wilkes
1940-41	Herbert W Wilkes
1941-42	W E Marston
1942-43	Alexander Comley
1943-44	Irvon Sunderland
1944-45	Clarence Wintle
1945-46	G Howard Heaton
1946-47	Gordon R Matthews

1947-48	Peter A G Osler MA
1948-49	J C S Branson
1949-50	William C Cheshire
1950-51	Frank Blennerhassett QC
1951-52	David P S Lowe LL B
1952-53	C C Bason
1953-54	James Ferriday
1954-55	R H Hopkins
1955-56	D C Norman
1956-57	Spencer A Comley
1957-58	George A E Craig JP
1958-59	Edwin H Cutts
1959-60	John F F Freeman
1960-61	Charles W Massey
1961-62	Charles Whitehead
1962-63	Robert Gaukroger
1963-64	Kenneth A Wilkinson
1964-65	Thomas Payne
1965-66	Donald C Wasdell
1966-67	H Banner Adkins
1967-68	Spencer A Comley
1968-69	Edwin H Cutts
1969-70	Kenneth A Wilkinson
1970-71	N John Masterton
1971-72	N John Masterton
1972-73	N John Masterton
1973-74	Anthony J Houghton
1974-75	Anthony J Houghton
1975-76	Roger V Stone
1976-77	William D Moyle
1977-78	Phillip C Couse
1978-79	Donald C Wasdell
1979-80	Alan M Harrison
1980-81	John C Coward
1981-82	Brian J Vertigen
1982-83	Roger W Hatton
1983-84	Christopher J Tuffs
1984-85	Geoffrey A Crofts
1985-86	Roger J Winter

1986-87	Dr Anthony P Joseph
1987-88	Raymond N Burton
1988-89	Raymond N Burton
1989-90	Raymond J Burn
1990-91	David M Slade
1991-92	Philip R Lesser
1992-93	Edward C Behague
1993-94	Reginald A G Willsher
1994-95	Antony Grazier
1995-96	Antony Grazier
1996-97	Richard M Cliff
1997-98	Timothy Ryan
1998-99	Anthony J Ridgway
1999-2000	Philip Gretton
2000-01	Peter Barnett
2001-02	Richard Tudor
2002-03	Richard Tudor
2003-04	Geoffrey Oakley
2004-05	Ian Marshall
2005-06	James Fergus
2006-07	Stephen Gilmore

Honorary secretaries

Where more than one name appears in a year, the office of honorary secretary was handed over during the session. There were elected three co-secretaries in 1864-65 and joint secretaries in 1888-90. In recent years, there have been separate dinner secretaries and debates secretaries. These are not listed.

Honorary secretaries of the Edgbaston Debating Society

1846-47	John C Barlow
1847-48	Alfred Wills/Edward Peyton
1848-49	Edmund K Blyth/Edward Peyton
1849-50	J H Howard Harris
1850-51	Robert Coad
1851-52	William Hudson/Robert Francis Martineau
1852-54	Charles E Mathews
1854-55	John Walford
1855	John Green

John Green had served for no more than a month when he became the honorary secretary of the amalgamated society.

Honorary secretary of the first Birmingham Debating Society

1848-50	John F Winfield

No records exist of the first Birmingham Debating Society prior to 1848. It is probable that John F Winfield, who was also honorary treasurer, took office from 1846 when the society was formed.

Honorary secretaries of the second Birmingham Debating Society

1850-52	George Jabet
1852-54	William S Allen
1854-55	John Pemberton Turner

Honorary secretaries of the Birmingham & Edgbaston Debating Society

1855-56	John Green
1856-57	George James Johnson
1857-58	Joseph Chirm
1858-59	Charles E Mathews
1859-60	Joseph Chamberlain
1861-63	George Spencer Mathews
1863-64	Herbert J Stack
1864-65	Alfred Browett/W C Osler/Thomas Anderton
1865-66	Alfred Browett
1866-68	Alfred Caddick
1868-71	Howard S Smith
1871-73	W H Ryland
1873-74	Walter Hornblower
1874-76	Arthur J Phillp
1876-78	Francis Lowe
1878-81	Edward H Lee
1881-82	S N Soloman
1882-83	W Fowler Carter
1883-85	Charles F Brown
1885-87	Edward Bickerton Williams
1887-88	Arthur L Jenkyn-Brown
1888-89	Cecil Crosskey/Montague Fordham
1889-90	Cecil Crosskey
1890-92	Thomas W Ryland
1892-94	S D Balden
1894-96	Arthur D Brooks
1896-97	C Lakin Smith
1897-99	Gardner Tyndall
1899-1900	Siward James
1900-01	Bertram G Grimley
1901-03	Bertram O Pemberton
1903-04	G Benyon Harris
1904-07	A R Rann
1907-09	Fitz-James Sawyer
1909-11	L Arthur Smith
1911-13	Gerald Botteley
1913-14	R Hill Norris

1914-16	M S Corby
1916-19	G Austin Baker
1919-22	Thomas H Varcoe
1922-24	Norman Wall
1924-25	R Wynne Frazier
1925-27	Hubert W Neep
1927-28	Kenneth Wood
1928-30	John F Bourke
1930-32	Herbert W Wilkes
1932-35	F L Blofeld
1935-38	C Peter Clarke
1938-42	Thomas Dornan
1942-45	G Howard Heaton
1945-46	L F Daniels
1946-48	Francis Bromilow
1948-49	David P S Lowe
1949-50	David P S Lowe/M R Roach
1950-51	Spencer Comley
1951-52	James Ferriday
1952-53	R Wollaston
1953-54	D C Norman
1954-55	James Bowker
1955-57	Dr J E Keen
1957-61	Robert Gaukroger
1961-63	Donald C Wasdell
1963-67	Roger V Stone
1967-69	Brian Janson-Smith
1969-72	Charles Whitehead
1972-74	Roger V Stone
1974-77	Anthony Biddle
1977-81	Brian J Vertigen
1981-82	John Taylor
1982-86	Raymond N Burton
1986-89	David M Slade
1989-91	Derek Beanland
1991-96	Michael Holt
1996-98	Conrad Charles
1998-2001	Bill Caswell
2001-04	Geoffrey Burcher
2004-	Roger V Stone

BIBLIOGRAPHY

The Victorians by A N Wilson
After the Victorians by A N Wilson
The British Revolution 1880-1939 by Robert Rhodes James
Birmingham Working People by George J Barnsby
A History of Birmingham by Chris Upton
History of Birmingham volume I by Conrad Gill
History of Birmingham volume II by Asa Briggs
English Social History by G M Trevelyan
A History of Our Own Times by Justin McCarthy
English Saga by Arthur Bryant
The Life of Neville Chamberlain by Keith Feiling
The History of The Leamington Tennis Court Club 1846-1996 by Charles Wade
The English by Jeremy Paxman
Radical Joe: A Life of Joseph Chamberlain by Denis Judd
Modern Birmingham and its Institutions by Dr J A Langford
Joseph Chamberlain: Entrepreneur in Politics by Peter T Marsh
Life of Joseph Chamberlain by J L Garvin

RULES OF THE SOCIETY

Adopted by an EGM on 13 November 1985, amended on 23 October 1996 and corrected in October 1999, and by a further amendment to Rule 3 by an EGM on 18 October 2000.

NATURE OF THE SOCIETY

1 The Society shall be called 'The Birmingham and Edgbaston Debating Society' and its objects shall be the debate of literary, political, historical, social and other subjects.

OF THE MEMBERS

2 Candidates for admission into the Society shall be aged at least eighteen years and shall be proposed and seconded in writing to the Secretary by members to whom they are personally known and, on sufficient notice of such nomination being given, there shall be published the names of the candidates with their proposers and seconders in the circular convening the ordinary meeting next following and a ballot shall be taken at that meeting. Prospective members shall be required to attend at least two meetings of the Society before their candidature be considered.

3 No candidate for admission into the Society shall be considered as elected if more than one third of votes given by the members present be unfavourable. A candidate who has been rejected shall not be eligible again to be a candidate until twelve months after such rejection.

4 Members shall pay an annual subscription of such an amount to be determined at each annual general meeting of the Society. This subscription shall be due and payable immediately following that meeting or, in the case of a new member, on election. Any members

neglecting to pay a subscription after a second application therefore has been made shall become liable to expulsion from the Society at the discretion of the committee. The committee shall have the power to reinstate such a member on immediate payment of all amounts due to the date of reinstatement.

5   All resignations from the Society must be made in writing and sent to the Secretary or the Treasurer.

6   Every member shall have the right to introduce visitors to ordinary meetings of the Society, unless the circular convening the meeting states otherwise. Visitors so introduced shall be allowed to speak on the subject of discussion and to vote thereon as hereafter indicated but they shall take no other part in the proceedings of the meeting.

OF THE OFFICERS AND COMMITTEE

7 (a) The officers of the Society shall be the President, Vice-President, Treasurer, Secretary, Dinner Secretary and Debates Secretary.

   (b) The committee shall consist of the officers and up to six members of the Society, four shall form a quorum.

8 (a) The officers and other members of the committee and auditor shall be elected at the annual general meeting, which shall be held before 1st December each year. Three clear days notice of all nominations shall be given to the Secretary in writing and in every case the proposer and seconder (who shall both be members of the Society) shall have their candidate's permission.

   (b) Any election shall be by ballot if demanded by one member.

   (c) If during the year a vacancy occurs in the committee, or amongst the officers, the committee may themselves appoint a member to fill such a vacancy.

9   In summoning the annual general meeting the Secretary shall print in the circular a copy of Rule 8 (a).

10 The committee shall have the power to arrange the subject of debate, to fix the date and time for any meeting of the Society, and generally to regulate the Society's proceedings, but not to admit new members or to make any alteration in or additional to the Rules of the Society.

11 The committee shall prepare annually a report of the Society's proceedings during the year, which shall be available for adoption at the next annual general meeting. The Treasurer's statement of accounts shall form part of that report.

OF THE CHAIR

12 The Chairman of each meeting shall be the President or, in his absence, the Vice-President. Should both these officers be absent, a Chairman for that meeting shall be nominated by the President or the officers present.

13 The Chairman shall have absolute authority in every question of order, shall be sole interpreter of the Rules, and in all cases of an equality of votes shall have a casting vote.

OF THE MEETINGS

14 The Society shall meet not less than six times in each year.

15 For the transaction of business at any meeting the presence of six members shall be necessary.

16 (a) At the close of the debate the Chairman shall put the resolution to the Meeting, permitting only members to vote and the vote shall be taken by show of hands first for and then against the resolution. On the occasion of a joint debate with another society or organisation shall be eligible to vote pari passu with members of the Society.

(b) The Chairman shall then take another vote, in which visitors shall be allowed to participate with members, but such second vote shall not influence the result of the first vote which shall be decisive.

17   The Secretary shall keep minutes of each meeting of the Society and of the committee and in the minutes shall be recorded the name of the Chairman, the names of those members present, the total attendance of members and visitors, the business transacted, the subject debated, the names of the speakers on each side, and the votes cast at the close of the debate. The secretary will deposit with the Birmingham Reference Library records of the Society, i.e. minute books, copies of the annual report and membership registers.

18   No amendment shall be allowed upon the subject arranged for debate.

19   Except when the Chairman shall decide otherwise before the commencement of a debate, the time allowed to each opener shall not exceed twenty minutes, and to each subsequent speaker five minutes.

20   No members shall be allowed to speak twice on the subject of debate (except by way of explanation or information) but the openers in the negative and affirmative shall each be permitted to make a reply of not more than ten minutes at the conclusion of the debate.

21   Any member who undertakes to speak as an opener but for whatever reason is prevented from doing so, shall provide a substitute.

22   The Secretary or such other member as deputed by the President shall give not less than seven day's notice of meetings of the Society.

OF THE RULES

23   Any motion involving alteration in or addition to the Rules of the Society or otherwise affecting its permanent constitution shall only be made at an extraordinary general meeting which only members may attend. The Secretary shall convene an extraordinary general meeting if required to do so by at least three members, and shall issue the circular convening such extraordinary general meeting not less than twenty one days before it is due to take place. The circular shall include the terms of the motion to be discussed, and such motion shall be accepted or rejected by the vote of the extraordinary general meeting.

24   No motion under Rule 23 shall be declared carried unless two thirds of the total votes cast are in favour of it.

25   Should all those members who have given notice of the motion be absent from the extraordinary general meeting at the time when the motion is called, it shall not be discussed or brought forward again, until after the next annual general meeting. In these circumstances the expense of the meeting shall be paid by the proposing members.

26   No alteration made in the Rules of the Society shall be reconsidered during the year in which the alteration was made, nor shall any motion proposed with the object of making an alteration in the Rules of the Society be considered again during the year in which it has been defeated.

27   The Secretary shall send to new members, upon their election, a copy of the Rules valid at that time, together with such other information about the Society as the committee may consider appropriate.

OF WINDING UP

28   In the event of the Society winding up, the committee shall be charged with delivering for safe keeping the records of the Society to the Birmingham Reference Library and the artefacts of the Society to the City of Birmingham Museum and Art Gallery.

29   Any surplus monies remaining after winding up the affairs of the Society shall be applied by the committee in the promotion and development of any like society sharing objects similar to those set out in Rule 1.